Being Disciples
of Jesus

A Guided Discovery for Groups and Individuals

Stephen J. Binz

LOYOLAPRESS.

CHICAGO

LOYOLAPRESS.

3441 N. ASHLAND AVENUE
CHICAGO, ILLINOIS 60657
(800) 621-1008
WWW.LOYOLABOOKS.ORG

Nihil Obstat	*Imprimatur*
Reverend John G. Lodge, S.S.L., S.T.D.	Reverend John F. Canary, D.Min.
Censor Deputatus	Vicar General
April 17, 2006	Archdiocese of Chicago
	April 18, 2006

The *Nihil Obstat* and *Imprimatur* are official declarations that a book is free of doctrinal and moral error. No implication is contained therein that those who have granted the *Nihil Obstat* and *Imprimatur* agree with the content, opinions, or statements expressed. Nor do they assume any legal responsibility associated with publication.

The excerpt from Dietrich Bonhoeffer (p. 35) is taken from his book *The Cost of Discipleship* (New York: Touchstone, 1995).

"The Minor Gospel Characters as Model Disciples" (p. 50–53) is taken from excerpts from Stephen J. Binz, *People of the Passion*, Threshold Bible Study (Mystic, CT: Twenty-Third Publications, 2004).

The quotation from Pope Gregory the Great (pp. 79) is taken from *Homilies on the Gospels*, by Bede the Venerable. Translated by Lawrence T. Martin and David Hurst (Collegeville, MN: Cistercian, 1993).

Interior design by Kay Hartmann/Communique Design
Illustration by Anni Betts

ISBN-13: 978-0-8294-2355-6
ISBN-10: 0-8294-2355-9

Printed in the United States of America
06 07 08 09 10 11 Bang 10 9 8 7 6 5 4 3 2 1

Contents

How to Use This Guide

If you want to learn how to be a follower of Jesus Christ, the natural place to begin is the Bible. Because the Holy Spirit guided the authors of Scripture, the book they wrote is an always-fresh source of wisdom and inspiration for walking along the way of discipleship.

In this book we will read excerpts from the Gospels of Matthew, Mark, Luke, and John to learn what these writers tell us about following Jesus. As we proceed, we will explore connections between what we find in Scripture, in the history of the Church, and our own lives today. The goal is to become more genuinely and consciously a part of the community of disciples who have followed Jesus through the ages.

Our approach will be a *guided discovery*. It will be *guided* because we all need support in understanding Scripture and reflecting on what it means for our lives. Scripture was written to be understood and applied in the community of faith, so we read the Bible *for* ourselves but not *by* ourselves. Even if we are reading alone rather than in a group, we need resources that help us grow in understanding. Our approach is also one of *discovery,* because each of us needs to encounter Scripture for ourselves and consider its meaning for our life. No one can do this for us.

This book is designed to give you both guidance for understanding and tools for discovery.

The introduction on page 6 will guide your reading by providing background material and helping you get oriented to the subject of our exploration. Each week, a brief "Background" section will give you context for the reading, and the "Exploring the Theme" section that follows the reading will bring out the meaning of the Scripture passages. Supplementary material between sessions will offer further resources for understanding.

The main tool for discovery is the "Questions for Reflection and Discussion" section in each session. The first questions in this section are designed to spur you to notice things in the text, sharpen your powers of observation, and read for comprehension. Other questions suggest ways to compare the people, situations, and experiences in the biblical texts with your own life and the world today—an important step toward grasping what God is saying to you through the Scripture and what your response might be. Choose the questions you think will work best for you. Preparing to answer all the questions ahead of time is highly recommended.

We suggest that you pay particular attention to the final question each week, labeled "Focus question." This question points to an especially important issue about discipleship raised by the reading. You may find it difficult to answer this focus question briefly. Do leave enough time for everyone in the group to discuss it!

Other sections encourage you to take an active approach to your Bible reading and discussion. At the start of each session, "Questions to Begin" will help you break the ice and start talk flowing. Often these questions are light and have only a slight connection to the reading. After each Scripture reading, there is a suggested time for a "First Impression." This gives you a chance to express a brief, initial, personal response to the text. Each session ends with a "Prayer to Close" that suggests a way of expressing your response to God.

How long are the discussion sessions? We've assumed you will have about an hour and twenty minutes. If you have less time, you'll find that most of the elements can be shortened somewhat.

Is homework necessary? You will get the most out of your discussions if you read the weekly material and prepare your answers to the questions in advance of each meeting. If participants are not able to prepare, read the "Exploring the Theme" sections aloud at the points where they appear.

What about leadership? You don't have to be an expert in the Bible to lead a discussion. Choose one or two people to act as discussion facilitators, and have everyone in the group read "Suggestions for Bible Discussion Groups" (page 92) before beginning.

Does everyone need a guide? a Bible? Everyone in the group will need their own copy of this book. It contains the biblical texts, so a Bible is not absolutely necessary—but each person will find it useful to have one. You should have at least one Bible on hand for your discussions. (See page 96 for recommendations.)

Before you begin, take a look at the suggestions for Bible discussion groups (page 92) or individuals (page 95).

Following Jesus, Then and Now

Jesus must have had a captivating appeal that made lots of people want to follow in his way. Being called by Jesus and accepting the challenge to follow him radically changed the lives of his first disciples. Today, Jesus continues to issue the call to discipleship, and people continue to choose to follow him. Reading the Gospel accounts of Jesus' relationship with his disciples will challenge us to tackle the issues of discipleship—issues that deal with nothing less than the purpose and direction of our lives.

Each of the Gospels presents the call of the disciples at the beginning of Jesus' public life. Then the Gospels focus on the disciples' attempts to understand who Jesus is and what it means to be his followers. Through success and struggle, insight and misunderstanding, and triumph and failure, the disciples gradually come to know Jesus and commit their lives to following in his way. As we read the Gospels, we are challenged to place ourselves in the role of the disciples—to encounter Jesus Christ, to learn from him, to travel with him from Galilee to the cross, and to decide whether or not we want to be his disciples.

In the Old Testament, Israel was chosen to be the disciple of God. Through his prophet Isaiah, God said to his people, "I am the Lord your God, who teaches you for your own good, who leads you in the way you should go" (Isaiah 48:17). Through the psalmist, God said, "I will instruct you and teach you the way you should go" (Psalm 32:8). Throughout salvation history, God dwelt with Israel and was her divine teacher; Israel received God's instructions and followed in God's way.

God's prophets chose disciples to learn from them and to share in their mission. Elisha was the disciple of Elijah, and Baruch the disciple of Jeremiah. These disciples played a significant role by passing on their teachings, which have come down to us in the prophetic books. In Jesus' time, Jewish students chose rabbis to follow. The student would absorb the rabbi's teaching and imitate his life. Then after applying himself sufficiently, the disciple would himself become a rabbi.

New Testament discipleship of Jesus differed considerably from that of the followers of the prophets or the rabbis. Jesus chose his disciples: "You did not choose me but I chose you" (John 15:16). The disciple ideally remained committed to the person of Jesus throughout his life, always remaining a disciple. The task of the disciple was to proclaim Jesus—by word and by example. In these ways, the model for Christian discipleship is not the relationship of a follower to a prophet or rabbi, but the relationship of Israel to God. The disciple of Jesus was taught by Jesus, given a new way of life, and offered a new future.

In each week of this six-week exploration of Scripture, we will look at a different experience of discipleship. In the first week, we will examine Jesus' initial call for several people to follow him. We will look at what that call involved and the response of Jesus' first disciples. In the second week, we will examine the costs of discipleship. We will see how the disciples often misunderstood Jesus and what Jesus taught them about the demands of following him. In the third week, Peter's successes and failures will serve as an example of one man's struggle to be Jesus' disciple. In the fourth week, we will consider John, the beloved disciple, and see how his love for Jesus inspired his discipleship. In the fifth week, we will look at Mary Magdalene to learn what her faithful devotion to Jesus can teach us about following in his way. In the sixth and final week, we will discuss how Mary the mother of Jesus is an inspiration for model discipleship.

Discipleship today essentially means being a Christian— entering into a lifelong relationship with Jesus. Today's disciples are challenged to do what Jesus did: teach, heal, take up the cross, and bring signs of God's kingdom into the world. Being a disciple of Jesus does not involve just an individual relationship with Jesus but also a bond of unity with the other disciples. It is a calling that embraces the whole of our human existence at every level. Discipleship involves both an interiorized spirituality and an external way of life. Let us enter the Gospels to explore what it means to be a disciple of Jesus, and then let us decide to answer the call and follow him.

THE CALL OF JESUS TO DISCIPLESHIP

Questions to Begin

10 minutes
Use a question or two to get warmed up for the reading.

---

1 What was it like for you to leave home to begin a new phase of your life?

---

2 When you go on a journey, do you usually pack too much or leave things behind?

Keep your eyes on the one who refused to turn stones into bread, jump from great heights, or rule with great temporal power. . . . Keep your eyes on the one who is poor with the poor, weak with the weak, and rejected with the rejected. That one is the source of all peace.

Henri Nouwen, *World Vision* magazine

Opening the Bible

10 minutes
Read the passage aloud. Let individuals take turns reading paragraphs.

The Background

What does it mean to be a disciple of Jesus Christ? Mark explores this question for the Church in his own day, probably in first-century Rome. In doing so, he explores this question for people in every age who are seeking to understand what it means to be called by Jesus and to follow in his way. The fundamental quality of genuine discipleship is following Jesus wherever he leads. These passages from the early chapters of Mark's Gospel offer us several narratives in which Jesus calls people to discipleship, indicating that discipleship is rooted in his personal call. Of those who are called in these accounts, most accept the call to be with Jesus and share in his mission. One does not accept the call, indicating that discipleship can be refused. Mark challenges us to consider our own discipleship as we seek to follow in the way of Jesus in our age in history.

The Reading: Mark 1:16–20; 2:13–17; 3:13–19; 6:7–13; 10:17–31

Jesus Invites His First Disciples to Follow Him

1:16 As Jesus passed along the Sea of Galilee, he saw Simon and his brother Andrew casting a net into the sea—for they were fishermen. 17 And Jesus said to them, "Follow me and I will make you fish for people." 18 And immediately they left their nets and followed him. 19 As he went a little farther, he saw James son of Zebedee and his brother John, who were in their boat mending the nets. 20 Immediately he called them; and they left their father Zebedee in the boat with the hired men, and followed him.

Jesus Calls Levi the Tax Collector to Be His Disciple

2:13 Jesus went out again beside the sea; the whole crowd gathered around him, and he taught them. 14 As he was walking along, he saw

Levi son of Alphaeus sitting at the tax booth, and he said to him, "Follow me." And he got up and followed him.

15 And as he sat at dinner in Levi's house, many tax collectors and sinners were also sitting with Jesus and his disciples—for there were many who followed him. 16 When the scribes of the Pharisees saw that he was eating with sinners and tax collectors, they said to his disciples, "Why does he eat with tax collectors and sinners?" 17 When Jesus heard this, he said to them, "Those who are well have no need of a physician, but those who are sick; I have come to call not the righteous but sinners."

Jesus Chooses Twelve

3:13 He went up the mountain and called to him those whom he wanted, and they came to him. 14 And he appointed twelve, whom he also named apostles, to be with him, and to be sent out to proclaim the message, 15 and to have authority to cast out demons. 16 So he appointed the twelve: Simon (to whom he gave the name Peter); 17 James son of Zebedee and John the brother of James (to whom he gave the name Boanerges, that is, Sons of Thunder); 18 and Andrew, and Philip, and Bartholomew, and Matthew, and Thomas, and James son of Alphaeus, and Thaddaeus, and Simon the Cananaean, 19 and Judas Iscariot, who betrayed him.

Jesus Sends the Twelve Out on Mission

6:7 He called the twelve and began to send them out two by two, and gave them authority over the unclean spirits. 8 He ordered them to take nothing for their journey except a staff; no bread, no bag, no money in their belts; 9 but to wear sandals and not to put on two tunics. 10 He said to them, "Wherever you enter a house, stay there until you leave the place. 11 If any place will not welcome you and they refuse to hear you, as you leave, shake off the dust that is on your feet as a testimony against them." 12 So they went out and proclaimed that all should repent. 13 They cast out many demons, and anointed with oil many who were sick and cured them.

Jesus Calls a Rich Man to Follow Him

10:17 As he was setting out on a journey, a man ran up and knelt before him, and asked him, "Good Teacher, what must I do to inherit eternal life?" 18 Jesus said to him, "Why do you call me good? No one is good but God alone. 19 You know the commandments: 'You shall not murder; You shall not commit adultery; You shall not steal; You shall not bear false witness; You shall not defraud; Honor your father and mother.'" 20 He said to him, "Teacher, I have kept all these since my youth." 21 Jesus, looking at him, loved him and said, "You lack one thing; go, sell what you own, and give the money to the poor, and you will have treasure in heaven; then come, follow me." 22 When he heard this, he was shocked and went away grieving, for he had many possessions.

23 Then Jesus looked around and said to his disciples, "How hard it will be for those who have wealth to enter the kingdom of God!" 24 And the disciples were perplexed at these words. But Jesus said to them again, "Children, how hard it is to enter the kingdom of God! 25 It is easier for a camel to go through the eye of a needle than for someone who is rich to enter the kingdom of God." 26 They were greatly astounded and said to one another, "Then who can be saved?" 27 Jesus looked at them and said, "For mortals it is impossible, but not for God; for God all things are possible."

28 Peter began to say to him, "Look, we have left everything and followed you." 29 Jesus said, "Truly I tell you, there is no one who has left house or brothers or sisters or mother or father or children or fields, for my sake and for the sake of the good news, 30 who will not receive a hundredfold now in this age—houses, brothers and sisters, mothers and children, and fields with persecutions—and in the age to come eternal life. 31 But many who are first will be last, and the last will be first."

First Impression

5 minutes
Briefly mention a question you have about the reading or one thing in it that surprised, impressed, delighted, or challenged you. No discussion! Just listen to one another's reactions.

Exploring the Theme

If participants have not read this section already, read it aloud. Otherwise go on to "Questions for Reflection and Discussion."

1:16–20. While he was passing along the Sea of Galilee, Jesus issued a personal call to four fishermen, Peter and Andrew (verses 16–18) and James and John (verses 19–20). While they were engaged in the ordinary routine of their lives—casting and mending their nets—Jesus offered them a clear invitation: "Follow me." These men did not come to Jesus asking to sign up; they were not volunteers. Jesus took the initiative. They were chosen not through any merit of their own. Their call was pure, unexpected grace—a gift from God.

This is the way it always is with God. Why did he choose a slave in Egypt (Moses) to form the Hebrews into a nation? a widow from Moab (Ruth) to prepare for Israel's monarchy? a young girl from Nazareth (Mary) to bring the Messiah? Why choose Israel out of all the peoples of the earth? God's invitation is not something one earns; it comes freely from God. Over and over God seems to choose the least likely candidates.

The chosen disciples immediately leave everything behind to follow Jesus. The spontaneous clarity of their response will contrast with the ambiguity of their response later in the Gospel, when the challenges of discipleship become great. Here they place their fate and future into the hands of the master. Jesus and his mission—the proclamation of God's kingdom—become the new focus of their lives.

Jesus himself is the fisherman here, and the four men are the fish. Jesus casts his word and they are caught up into the reign of God. Jesus calls them in turn to fish for people on this deeper level. "I will make you fish for people," Jesus says, inviting them to share in his mission. Through their work, others will be caught up into God's reign and follow Jesus.

For us, as for them, the heart of discipleship lies in following Jesus. His call is the invitation to make him and his mission our life's first priority. As we study the first disciples of Jesus, we are challenged to ask ourselves where our hearts lie. Is Jesus at the center or merely at the periphery? Is Jesus truly the one we follow, the master of our hearts and our lives?

2:13–17. The call of Levi shares many similarities with the call of the first four disciples. While he was walking along the lake,

Jesus saw Levi engaged in the ordinary routine of his life. Jesus issued the personal invitation, "Follow me," and Levi got up and followed him immediately. Like the four fishermen, Levi separated himself from his daily occupation to form a personal attachment to Jesus and join him on his way.

Mark inserts this account into his narrative to make a point about the kind of people who followed Jesus as his disciples. Tax collecting was considered a despicable occupation by first-century Jews. "Tax collectors and sinners," a phrase used three times in verses 15 and 16, indicates those groups that were ostracized from Jewish society. The fact that Jesus calls his followers from among the outcasts, and even eats with them, was scandalous. Mark adds an explanatory note to the description of Jesus' table companions— "for there were many who followed him" (2:15)—indicating that by now Jesus had a large number of followers and that some of them were former tax collectors and sinners.

Those Jesus called were certainly not holier or more capable than anyone else. The fact that Jesus called fishermen and tax collectors indicates that discipleship is not something for which we need to qualify. Jesus called sinners and brought them healing and forgiveness (2:17). He is willing to touch us precisely where we think we are most untouchable.

3:13–19. The core of Jesus' disciples were twelve in number. Jesus calls those whom he chooses. The Twelve are not more qualified than others; the only difference is that Jesus has called them. The unconditional response of the Twelve is captured by the phrase "and they came to him."

There are two parts to the disciples' commission: "to be with him" and "to be sent out" (3:14). These are not two distinct activities but two inseparable aspects of the one call. Being with Jesus and being sent by him is the life of a disciple in a nutshell. Those called to follow were to be the steady companions of Jesus, living with him, being formed by him, and identifying their lives with his. Only then could they be sent out to serve, to continue his mission. We too must come to know and love Jesus intimately before we can continue his work and bring others to him.

The call to discipleship is not a private companionship with him; it is a call to community. The twelve disciples are a motley and diverse group. Greek names like Philip and Andrew are mixed with Hebrew names like Simon and Matthew. There are the "Sons of Thunder" and Simon "the rock" and Judas the betrayer. We are told in other Gospels that Matthew is a tax collector, and thus a supporter of Roman domination, and Simon is a zealot, which probably means that he is an opponent of Rome. The two men represent opposite extremes in Jewish society at this time. Jesus calls different, unique individuals to form a community of disciples.

6:7–13. The twelve disciples who were called to "be with" Jesus and to join him in ministry are now sent out. Discipleship always has a missionary dimension. It is not simply an interior spiritual quest. The Twelve went out and proclaimed the Good News by preaching, teaching, exorcizing demons, and anointing the sick with oil for their healing.

Jesus told them to "take nothing for their journey except a staff" (6:8). They must travel light because of the urgency of their mission and their need to rely on God alone to accomplish it. Not finding security in themselves, they must learn to trust completely in God. When people refuse to hear or receive their message, they must not tarry, seeking to persuade them, but must move on. The mission belongs to God.

10:17–31. Again, while Jesus is journeying, he issues an invitation: "Come, follow me" (10:21). But this time the call is refused. When Jesus issues his call to radical discipleship, the rich man goes away shocked and grieving—"for he had many possessions" (10:22).

The wealthy man seemed sincere in his desire for eternal life (10:17). He had followed the commandments since his youth. But Jesus told him that more is necessary than obeying the teachings of the law. The man could attain his goal only by selling what he had, giving to the poor, and following him. Jesus' reply falls on the astonished man's ears in five urgent imperatives: go, sell, give, come, and follow.

Jesus does not require every disciple in every age to give up their possessions and embrace poverty. The cost of discipleship varies for each person. Yet would-be followers of Jesus must rid themselves of anything and everything that impedes their following Jesus wholeheartedly. Apparently this man's riches were the hindrance that kept him from committing himself completely to Jesus and devoting himself to the mission of God's reign.

Jesus turned from the rich man and spoke to his disciples about the obstacles to salvation created by possessions. The disciples were "perplexed" (10:24) and "astounded" (10:26) because their culture had understood wealth as a sign of God's blessings. Jesus never taught that wealth in itself is evil. But love of money, desire for possessions, and attachment to wealth can become an insurmountable hindrance to true discipleship.

The teachings of Jesus on the dangers of wealth for the life of discipleship are often explained in ways that make it less upsetting to our system of values. Yet we cannot escape the fact that Jesus speaks to us all when he quietly affirms that the fullness of life is found not in accumulating things but in disencumbering ourselves of them. If we are not shocked, grieved, perplexed, and astounded by this teaching, then we have not yet heard Jesus correctly.

Reflections. The foundation of Jesus' call to discipleship is radical commitment. Discipleship today means accepting the same call that Jesus issued to his original disciples—the call to follow him and allow him to be the master of our lives. As in the Gospels, our discipleship involves two elements: being with Jesus and being sent out by Jesus. Being with him means cultivating a relationship with him, listening to his word in Scripture, and encountering him through the sacraments of his Church. Being sent out by Jesus means witnessing him through the example of our lives, teaching gospel principles in our family and society, and extending his healing ministry to those in need. Like the disciples of the gospel, we must renounce everything that stands in the way of responding to his call wholeheartedly. Jesus continues to call disciples today. Our challenge is to allow his grace to open our hearts to him.

Questions for Reflection and Discussion

45 minutes
Choose questions according to your interest and time.

1 In what way is "fishing for people" a good metaphor for discipleship?

2 The fishermen might have been paying extorted and inflated taxes to Levi. How do you think the fishermen and tax collector got along as disciples?

3 In the Gospel accounts, Jesus doesn't call those we might expect: the educated, the religious, or those who are financially and socially successful. Why do you suppose this is?

4 What does it mean to you to be a disciple of Jesus Christ? In what way do you experience a personal calling from Jesus?

5 The disciples of Jesus were a mixed and varied group with totally different political perspectives and social backgrounds. In what ways does diversity present challenges to the community of Christ's disciples today?

6 Jesus charged his disciples to travel light while on their missionary journey. In what way does your Christian discipleship require you to simplify your life?

7 Jesus said that for mortals it is impossible to be saved, but "for God all things are possible" (10:27). Why is it impossible for us to earn salvation? Why is salvation best described as a gift?

8 The wealthy man's many possessions were the hindrance that prevented him from following Jesus. What hindrance stands in the way of your full commitment to discipleship?

9 For personal reflection: The teachings of Jesus concerning wealth shocked, grieved, perplexed, and astounded his disciples and the rich man. What is your response to this teaching?

10 **Focus question.** In what way do the two parts of the disciples' commission, "to be with him" and "to be sent out" (3:14), define the Christian life? In what specific ways do you feel called by Jesus to be with him and to be sent out?

Prayer to Close

10 minutes
Use this approach—or create your own!

♦ Slowly pray together the
following prayer by St. Philaret,
Metropolitan of Moscow.

My Lord, I don't know what I
    ought to ask of you.
You and you alone know my
    needs.
You love me more than I am able
    to love you.
O God, grant to me, your
    servant, all which I cannot
    ask.
For a cross I dare not ask, nor
    for consolation;
I dare only to stand in your
    presence.
My heart is open to you.
You see my needs of which I
    myself am unaware.
Behold and lift me up!
In your presence I stand,
awed and silenced by your will
    and your judgments,
into which my mind cannot
    penetrate.
To you I offer myself as a
    sacrifice.
No other desire is mine but to
    fulfill your will.
Teach me how to pray.
And may you yourself pray
    within me. Amen.

Living Tradition

The Corporal and Spiritual Works of Mercy

This section is a supplement for individual reading.

Jesus called his disciples to compassionate service. The forms of practical spiritual and physical service are traditionally categorized as spiritual and corporal works of mercy (see the *Catechism of the Catholic Church,* section 2447).

The corporal works of mercy. (1) *Feed the hungry.* Examples: Fasting to foster empathy with the poor, serving a meal to a hungry person, and working to improve economic and social structures so as to help eliminate poverty. (2) *Give drink to the thirsty.* Giving cool water to a thirsty person and providing unpolluted water for those who don't have access to it. (3) *Clothe the naked.* Offering sufficient clothing, bedding, and tools for labor; suggesting other ways of restoring dignity to those stripped of their self-respect. (4) *Shelter the homeless.* Offering a sense of belonging to the alienated, abused, and misunderstood; offering housing to migrants, refugees, orphans, and street people. (5) *Visit the sick.* Giving care and companionship to the ill, homebound, and elderly; meeting the needs of the physically and emotionally disabled. (6) *Visit the imprisoned.* Providing opportunities for education, job training, and spiritual and psychological counseling to the incarcerated; freeing victims of violence and injustice from psychological wounds. (7) *Bury the dead.* Providing companionship, grieving with the bereaved, and helping the dying to prepare for death.

The spiritual works of mercy. (1) *Admonish the sinner.* Offering advice to help a person turn from sin; setting a good example. (2) *Instruct the ignorant.* Correcting misunderstandings and prejudice based on ignorance and fear. (3) *Counsel the doubtful.* Giving helpful advice, good examples, and encouraging words to a person struggling with doubts about faith. (4) *Comfort the sorrowful.* Giving attention and empathy to the bereaved, lonely, and alienated. (5) *Bear wrongs patiently.* Responding with patience and understanding rather than retaliation to wrongs done to us, in order to prevent harm from escalating. (6) *Forgive all injuries.* Seeking to heal physical, mental, and verbal injury rather than becoming bitter, resentful, and vindictive. (7) *Pray for the living and the dead.* Offering intercessory prayer; asking the saints and angels to assist the living and the dead.

Between Discussions

The Three Movements of Discipleship

A disciple is a learner, a pupil who follows the way of a teacher. Jesus taught his disciples through the rhythm of his own life, which consisted essentially of three movements: quiet prayer, supportive community, and active service. Throughout his life, Jesus kept these three movements in balance. He taught his disciples to do the same.

Quiet prayer. All of the Gospels, especially Luke's Gospel, show Jesus habitually in prayer. It is primarily through the example of Jesus praying that his disciples learned the significance of solitary prayer, and it is through portraying Jesus in prayer that the Gospel writers teach future disciples how to make prayer a part of the rhythm of life.

Jesus spent time in prayer particularly at the critical points in his life. When Jesus was praying after his Baptism, the Holy Spirit descended on him and a voice from heaven said, "You are my Son, the Beloved" (Luke 3:21–22). This anointing by the Holy Spirit was a turning point for Jesus and marked the beginning of his public ministry proclaiming the reign of God.

When it came time for Jesus to choose the twelve who would be his closest disciples, he "went out to the mountain to pray; and he spent the night in prayer to God" (Luke 6:12). After this night of quiet prayer, Jesus chose his twelve disciples "when day came." Through his own example, Jesus showed his chosen ones the importance of turning to God in solitude to seek his will. He demonstrated that quiet prayer is essential when we are faced with important decisions or when we are at a turning point in our lives. Only in solitude can we know that we are God's beloved and become sensitive to the movements of God's Spirit guiding us in the face of critical decisions.

Later in his ministry, Jesus began to tell his disciples that his mission would involve laying down his life. His death would not be a random accident, but the culmination of his life of giving and loving. In quiet solitude Jesus prayed to the Father. While Luke does not tell us the content of his prayer, we may suppose that he spoke to his Father about his upcoming death and asked the Father to give his disciples understanding. Luke's Gospel relates this scene midway through Jesus' public life: "Once when Jesus was praying alone, with only the disciples near him," he asked them, "Who do you say that I am?" (Luke 9:18–20). Only through understanding his identity could they accept the necessity of his suffering. Jesus then went on to speak about the rejection, suffering, and death that his mission would entail. Like Jesus, disciples accept their identity and mission through quiet prayer in communion with God.

On the night before his death, Jesus went out to pray in a secluded area on the Mount of Olives "as was his custom" (Luke 22:39). As Jesus withdrew to pray, he urged his disciples to pray also. In solitude, Jesus abandoned his life into his Father's hands: "Not my will but yours be done" (22:42). We say the words *Thy will be done* when we pray the prayer that Jesus taught his followers, and we often say these words without a second thought. But there may be points in our lives when these words choke in our throats, when abandoning ourselves or our loved ones to the will of God takes everything we have. Jesus' prayer at the time of his looming death did not come easily for him either.

Jesus offered his last two prayers on the cross. He prayed for those responsible for his death, asking the Father to forgive them (Luke 23:34). And at the last moment he prayed, "Father, into your hands I commend my spirit" (Luke 23:46). In suffering and at the point of death, Jesus prayed to his loving Father, knowing that he was God's beloved. With this knowledge, renewed in solitary prayer, Jesus was able to give his own life and the lives of his persecutors into the hands of his Father. Jesus invites his disciples into the deep trust in God that comes from knowing that we are his beloved children. This trust can help us deal with a great amount of success and a great amount of failure without losing our true identity and our confidence in God.

Supportive community. So often, we try to do something ourselves. When that doesn't work, we go to others for help, and try to do it with a community. When that doesn't work, sometimes we start praying. But the order that Jesus teaches his disciples is the reverse. Discipleship begins by being with God in quiet prayer, then it creates a supportive community, and finally it goes out in active service of others.

After praying all night, Jesus chose his disciples. His solitary communion with God must have helped him realize his need and desire to share his mission with others. Jesus did not choose disciples because he couldn't do it on his own. He chose them because in his prayerful solitude before God he was moved to activate his divine mission through a community of disciples.

A community is not a group of people who think, talk, and act alike. That is called a club, a clique, or a social group. A community is a diverse group of people seeking to be faithful to an identity and a mission that they have been given. The community of disciples is the followers of Jesus seeking to be with him and to do what he did. The first community to gather around Jesus was composed of men and women who were far from similar; they were a collection of different, and often conflicting, personalities.

A healthy community must be founded on the solitary prayer of each individual. In quiet prayer before God, a person discovers his real identity and call. In the silence of God's presence, we discover that we are loved unconditionally by God. Only when we are comfortable in quiet with God will we be comfortable with others.

Whether our community is a religious order, parish, family, marriage, or friendship, we cannot expect another person to give us what only God can give. Another person cannot make us feel totally loved and satisfied. When we expect other people to do that for us, our relationships can only be resentful, manipulative, and demanding. Community cannot be formed with lonely people seeking out other lonely people. Only through being alone with God and knowing that we are loved can we become the kind of people who can form supportive and life-giving communities.

Active service. The first word of Jesus to his disciples was always *come*—come follow me, come learn from me, come to watch and listen. Only after they came to Jesus and lived with him and learned from him could he say, "Go." First, Jesus called the Twelve "to be with him," and only then could they "be sent out" (Mark 3:14).

Jesus sent out his disciples to preach and to heal—essentially, to do what he was doing. After being formed in prayer and community, the disciples were ready to share in the work of God's kingdom. Now they were able to be a community of disciples, proclaiming the Good News in word and deed, and serving humanity for the sake of the kingdom.

All disciples are called to active engagement in the world. Discipleship can never be simply a personal relationship between Jesus and me. As St. Teresa of Ávila said, it means being the hands and feet of Jesus, the eyes through which he looks with compassion on the world.

Jesus sends his disciples into the world for the same reason that he was sent into the world—for the salvation of people. Disciples are to be obedient to Jesus in the same way that Jesus was obedient to the Father. Genuine obedience has nothing to do with forced compliance or unthinking submission. In both Hebrew and Greek—languages in which Scripture is written—the word translated "obedience" is rooted in the verb *to listen.* Jesus listened intently to his Father in prayer and then responded with his life. He taught his disciples how to listen so that they could then continue his teaching and healing mission.

As disciples of Jesus, we are instruments of God's saving power in the world. We need to listen to him. If we listen to our own fears, to our desires for power, to the false messages of our world, and to those opposed to the way of love, we are failing to listen closely to Jesus. The disciples in the Gospels failed often because they did not listen to Jesus. They heard the other voices and they denied Jesus and fled from him when conditions became difficult. The way of discipleship means listening to Jesus, imitating him, following him, and taking up the cross.

The Cost of Discipleship

Questions to Begin

10 minutes
Use a question or two to get warmed up for the reading.

---

1 Which of your five senses would you miss the most if it were gone?

---

2 If you could bring back one aspect of childhood to your life today, what would it be? What part of childhood are you most glad you've outgrown?

How is the disciple to know what kind of cross is meant for him? He will find out as soon as he begins to follow his Lord and to share his life.

Dietrich Bonhoeffer, *The Cost of Discipleship*

10 minutes
Read the passage aloud. Let individuals take turns reading paragraphs.

The Background

In the middle of Mark's Gospel, Jesus begins to teach his disciples that he must suffer, die, and rise again. At the same time, he teaches them about the cost of discipleship. Each time Jesus predicts his own suffering and death, his words are met with misunderstanding and resistance on the part of his disciples. Jesus then takes the opportunity to teach them about the intimate connection between his own mission and what it means to be his disciple. This middle section of the Gospel is framed by two accounts of people whose sight is restored by Jesus: a blind man who gradually comes to see clearly (Mark 8:22–26) and a man who, after receiving his sight, follows Jesus (Mark 10:46–52). Throughout this section Jesus is trying to heal the spiritual blindness of his disciples—to open their eyes to the full meaning of being his disciples, so that they will be able to follow him.

The Reading: Mark 8:22–25, 29–35; 9:30–37; 10:32–52

Jesus Restores a Blind Man's Sight

8:22 They came to Bethsaida. Some people brought a blind man to him and begged him to touch him. 23 He took the blind man by the hand and led him out of the village; and when he had put saliva on his eyes and laid his hands on him, he asked him, "Can you see anything?" 24 And the man looked up and said, "I can see people, but they look like trees, walking." 25 Then Jesus laid his hands on his eyes again; and he looked intently and his sight was restored, and he saw everything clearly.

Jesus Teaches His Disciples to Take Up the Cross

8:29 [Jesus] asked them, "But who do you say that I am?" Peter answered him, "You are the Messiah." 30 And he sternly ordered them not to tell anyone about him. 31 Then he began to teach them that the Son of Man must undergo great suffering, and be rejected by the elders, the chief priests, and the scribes, and be killed, and after three days rise again. 32 He said all this quite openly. And Peter took him aside and began to rebuke him. 33 But turning and looking at his disciples, he rebuked Peter and said, "Get behind me, Satan! For you are setting your mind not on divine things but on human things."

34 He called the crowd with his disciples, and said to them, "If any want to become my followers, let them deny themselves and take up their cross and follow me. 35 For those who want to save their life will lose it, and those who lose their life for my sake, and for the sake of the gospel, will save it."

Jesus Teaches His Disciples to Be Servants of All

9:30 They went on from there and passed through Galilee. He did not want anyone to know it; 31 for he was teaching his disciples, saying to them, "The Son of Man is to be betrayed into human hands, and they will kill him, and three days after being killed, he will rise again." 32 But they did not understand what he was saying and were afraid to ask him.

33 Then they came to Capernaum; and when he was in the house he asked them, "What were you arguing about on the way?" 34 But they were silent, for on the way they had argued with one another who was the greatest. 35 He sat down, called the twelve, and said to them, "Whoever wants to be first must be last of all and servant of all." 36 Then he took a little child and put it among them; and taking it in his arms, he said to them, 37 "Whoever welcomes one such child in my name welcomes me, and whoever welcomes me welcomes not me but the one who sent me."

Jesus Teaches His Disciples the Cost of Discipleship

10:32 They were on the road, going up to Jerusalem, and Jesus was walking ahead of them; they were amazed, and those who followed were afraid. He took the twelve aside again and began to tell them what was to happen to him, 33 saying, "See, we are going up to Jerusalem, and the Son of Man will be handed over to the chief priests and the scribes, and they will condemn him to death; then they will hand him over to the Gentiles; 34 they will mock him, and spit upon him, and flog him, and kill him; and after three days he will rise again."

35 James and John, the sons of Zebedee, came forward to him and said to him, "Teacher, we want you to do for us whatever we ask of you." 36 And he said to them, "What is it you want me to do for you?" 37 And they said to him, "Grant us to sit, one at your right hand

and one at your left, in your glory." 38 But Jesus said to them, "You do not know what you are asking. Are you able to drink the cup that I drink, or be baptized with the baptism that I am baptized with?" 39 They replied, "We are able." Then Jesus said to them, "The cup that I drink you will drink; and with the baptism with which I am baptized, you will be baptized; 40 but to sit at my right hand or at my left is not mine to grant, but it is for those for whom it has been prepared."

41 When the ten heard this, they began to be angry with James and John. 42 So Jesus called them and said to them, "You know that among the Gentiles those whom they recognize as their rulers lord it over them, and their great ones are tyrants over them. 43 But it is not so among you; but whoever wishes to become great among you must be your servant, 44 and whoever wishes to be first among you must be slave of all. 45 For the Son of Man came not to be served but to serve, and to give his life a ransom for many."

A Blind Man Regains His Sight and Follows Jesus

10:46 They came to Jericho. As he and his disciples and a large crowd were leaving Jericho, Bartimaeus son of Timaeus, a blind beggar, was sitting by the roadside. 47 When he heard that it was Jesus of Nazareth, he began to shout out and say, "Jesus, Son of David, have mercy on me!" 48 Many sternly ordered him to be quiet, but he cried out even more loudly, "Son of David, have mercy on me!" 49 Jesus stood still and said, "Call him here." And they called the blind man, saying to him, "Take heart; get up, he is calling you." 50 So throwing off his cloak, he sprang up and came to Jesus. 51 Then Jesus said to him, "What do you want me to do for you?" The blind man said to him, "My teacher, let me see again." 52 Jesus said to him, "Go; your faith has made you well." Immediately he regained his sight and followed him on the way.

First Impression

5 minutes
Briefly mention a question you have about the reading or one thing in it that surprised, impressed, delighted, or challenged you. No discussion! Just listen to one another's reactions.

Exploring the Theme

If participants have not read this section already, read it aloud. Otherwise go on to "Questions for Reflection and Discussion."

8:22–25. In the account of the blind man, seeing has two levels of meaning: physical vision and inner understanding. In the passage immediately preceding this miracle, Jesus asks his disciples, "Do you have eyes, and fail to see?" (8:18) and "Do you not yet understand?" (8:21). The healing account introduces the section of Mark's Gospel in which Jesus teaches his disciples a deeper understanding of what it means to follow him. The healing of the blind man represents the gradual healing of the disciples' spiritual blindness—their failure to understand the mission of Jesus.

The healing of the blind man takes place in a two-stage process. Jesus first restores his sight, and then enables him to see clearly—to understand what he sees. For his disciples, Jesus enables them to see and understand, first by experiencing the call to discipleship and then by gradually coming to understand the cost of discipleship. All of us can identify with the slow but sure process of coming to understand Jesus, in which things sometimes look blurry but become clearer as we follow him.

8:29–35. All would-be followers of Jesus must answer the question that Jesus asked his original disciples: "Who do you say that I am?" (8:29). Peter's answer—"You are the Messiah" (8:29)—is correct but incomplete. Jesus is truly the Messiah, but not according to the prevalent Jewish expectation of the time, in which the Messiah would be a triumphant warrior. Hence Jesus tells his disciples not to publicly hail him as the Messiah (8:30).

The disciples have reached the first stage of understanding, yet their picture of Jesus is hazy and blurred. The second stage of their coming to understand Jesus is about to begin, where Jesus will correct their inadequate understandings of his identity and help them understand the implications for their discipleship.

Jesus asks his crucial question in Caesarea Philippi, north of Galilee. He will teach his disciples the implications of calling him the Messiah as he walks with them along the way from north to south, from Galilee to Jerusalem. Through supplying geographical references for incidents and reminding us that the disciples were "on the way," Mark presents the process of their coming to understand Jesus as a journey. At the end of the journey—at the cross in Jerusalem—Jesus can be understood fully and the implications of following him are starkly clear.

Following Peter's response that Jesus is the Messiah, Jesus offers a series of three predictions (in chapters 8, 9, and 10) in which he teaches his disciples that he must be rejected, suffer, die, and then rise from the dead. Following each of these predictions, the disciples fail to understand and accept his teaching. Confronted with the repeated failures of the disciples to truly "see," Jesus offers three teachings on what discipleship entails.

Peter is unable to accept the idea that the Messiah would suffer, and he responds to Jesus' prediction of his own suffering with a protest (8:32). Peter tries to talk Jesus out of the necessity of suffering, and Jesus strongly rebukes him. Jesus declares that Peter is like Satan, in the sense that he is trying to tempt him away from his mission.

Jesus responds to Peter's failure to understand the mystery of the cross by offering his first teaching on the meaning of discipleship. We would like a Messiah who would bring us nothing but happiness, victory, and bliss. Are we ready to follow one who promises us a share in his suffering?

The call to follow Jesus, first issued to Peter and to the others along a beautiful lake in Galilee, is now defined in the shadow of the cross. Jesus offers a threefold description of discipleship: denying oneself, taking up one's cross, and following in Jesus' way (8:34). The call to take up one's cross means that a disciple must be ready to undergo suffering and possibly even death. The way to reach self-fulfillment is by practicing self-denial. Losing one's life for the sake of Christ and the gospel is the way to save one's life (8:35). Followers of Jesus must love Jesus and the gospel more than their own lives.

9:30–37. Jesus gave his followers a second prediction of his passion as he "passed through Galilee" on his way to Jerusalem (9:30–31). Once again they are baffled by his words (9:32).

Their total incomprehension of all that Jesus has taught them about his fate and what it means to follow him is seen in their argument with one another about who is the greatest (9:34). This concern for their own prestige and advancement shows how far they are from discipleship, in which self-denial and taking up the cross are the foremost characteristics.

Jesus again responds to their failure to understand by offering teaching. He says that "whoever wants to be first must be last of all and servant of all" (9:35). As a visual aid, Jesus embraces a child. He tells his disciples that "whoever welcomes one such child in my name welcomes me" (9:37). Since a child had no social status or power in the Greco-Roman culture, Jesus is saying that serving the powerless and helpless is an indication of genuine discipleship. Followers of Jesus are called to serve the lowly and assist those in need. Jesus turns the perspective of the world upside down: true greatness means giving ourselves in service, especially to those from whom we can receive no benefit in return.

10:32–45. Jesus' third prediction of his suffering is given as he and his disciples are "going up to Jerusalem." As Jesus walks ahead of them with firm determination, the disciples are amazed and afraid. Again, they fail to comprehend what he is saying, and they fail to understand their call to share in his suffering.

The request of James and John for places to the right and left of Jesus highlights the disciples' miserable misunderstanding. Despite Jesus' threefold prediction of his own suffering and death in Jerusalem, the disciples still fantasize about the coming glory and scheme for positions of privilege. The irony of their request is that the positions to the right and left of Jesus will be occupied by the two robbers crucified with Jesus. He will be enthroned as king, but his throne will be a cross, and his crown will be made of thorns. When the other ten hear of the request of James and John, they are angry (10:41)—not with moral indignation at the ambition of the other two, but because they want the best places for themselves.

Again the failure of the disciples to understand prompts Jesus' teaching on the nature of discipleship. True greatness, he says, involves serving others. In fact, the greatest person will be the one who serves others the most (10:43–44)—a dramatic reversal of the world's standards. This servant leadership is modeled on

Jesus himself, who came to serve and to give his life (10:45). Those who contemplate following Jesus must serve as he served, offering themselves for the sake of others.

10:46–52. The middle section of Mark's Gospel began with the healing of a blind man, and Jesus now heals another blind man as his journey draws to an end. These healings are parables in action, hinting that the eyes of Jesus' followers will eventually be opened. The question of Jesus to the blind man, "What do you want me to do for you?" (10:51), echoes the question he asked of James and John (10:36). The blind man's enlightened answer corrects their misguided request.

The healing of Bartimaeus took place at Jericho. From here, it was only a short distance up to Jerusalem, but a steep and rugged climb. Mark notes that Bartimaeus followed Jesus "on the way" (10:52), which certainly means that the healed man followed him up to Jerusalem. It also means that Bartimaeus followed Jesus on the way of Christian discipleship, the way of the cross.

Reflections. Three times along the way from north to south, Jesus tried to open the eyes of his spiritually blind disciples. And three times these disciples failed to understand the necessity of his suffering and the meaning of their discipleship. Only at the cross can the identity of Jesus be fully understood and the meaning of discipleship comprehended. As we reflect on the challenges of our lives in light of the Scriptures, Jesus will heal our blindness and open our eyes to the full significance of discipleship. He calls us, like his original disciples, to take up the cross and walk with him along the way from suffering into life.

Questions for Reflection and Discussion

45 minutes
Choose questions according to your interest and time.

1 How would you explain the difference between the three characteristics of genuine discipleship offered by Jesus in Mark 8:34?

2 Compare the two accounts of the blind men at the beginning and end of this section. What similarities and differences do you find? Why do you suppose Mark placed them in this order?

3 What is the motivation of James and John in making their request? How does their request reflect a kind of blindness?

4 How do you answer the question of Jesus "Who do you say that I am?" How can answering the question "Who is Jesus?" lead you to a clearer answer to the question "Who am I?"

5 In what way have you experienced being a disciple of Jesus as a journey? Where has he led you so far? Where are you going?

6 What aspects of Jesus' teaching run contrary to popular values and ideals today?

7 What is your understanding of greatness? Is generous service to others a part of your concept of greatness? Who do you consider to be examples of a person giving generous service to others?

8 **Focus question.** What is the most challenging aspect of Jesus' teaching for you? Do some of his standards seem impossible to you? To what degree are you willing to let Jesus redirect your life?

Prayer to Close

10 minutes
Use this approach—or create your own!

♦ Begin by asking each person to think of one word or phrase from the discussion that stands out to them. Ask each one in turn to state their word or phrase followed by a moment of silence.

Divide the group in two and alternately pray Paul's words in Philippians 2:3–8. End with an Our Father.

I. Do nothing from selfish ambition or conceit, but in humility regard others as better than yourselves.

II. Let each of you look not to your own interests, but to the interests of others.

I. Let the same mind be in you that was in Christ Jesus, who, though he was in the form of God, did not regard equality with God as something to be exploited,

II. but emptied himself, taking the form of a slave, being born in human likeness.

I. And being found in human form, he humbled himself and became obedient to the point of death—

II. even death on a cross.

Saints in the Making

Dietrich Bonhoeffer and the Cost of Discipleship

This section is a supplement for individual reading.

Dietrich Bonhoeffer, a young German Lutheran pastor, was arrested by the Gestapo in 1943 because he had joined the underground, convinced that it was his duty as a Christian to work for Hitler's defeat. In prisons and concentration camps, all those who came in contact with him were inspired by his indomitable courage, his unselfishness, and his pastoral care offered to his sick, anxious, and depressed fellow prisoners. Some of his prison guards became so attached to him that they smuggled out of prison his papers and poems written there. He was executed at the concentration camp at Flossenbürg, Germany, on April 9, 1945, just a few days before it was liberated by the Allies. The following excerpt is from his book *The Cost of Discipleship.*

The cross is laid on every Christian. The first Christ-suffering which every man must experience is the call to abandon the attachment of this world. It is that dying of the old man which is the result of his encounter with Christ. As we embark upon discipleship we surrender ourselves to Christ in union with his death—we give over our lives to death. Thus it begins; the cross is not the terrible end to an otherwise god-fearing and happy life, but it meets us at the beginning of our Communion with Christ. When Christ calls a man, he bids him come and die. . . .

If we refuse to take up our cross and submit to suffering and rejection at the hands of men, we forfeit our fellowship with Christ and have ceased to follow him. But if we lose our lives in his service and carry our cross, we shall find our lives again in the fellowship of the cross with Christ.

Discipleship means allegiance to the suffering Christ, and it is therefore not at all surprising that Christians should be called upon to suffer. In fact it is a joy and a token of his grace. The acts of the early Christian martyrs are full of evidence which shows how Christ transfigures for his own the hour of their mortal agony by granting them the unspeakable assurance of his presence. In the hour of the cruellest torture they bear for his sake, they are made partakers in the perfect joy and bliss of fellowship with him.

Between Discussions

The Three Disciplines of Discipleship

The word *disciple* and the word *discipline* are very similar because they have the same root, a Latin word that means "to learn." If a disciple is a learner, a pupil who follows the way of a teacher, then what a disciple learns is the master's way—the master's discipline. If we want to be disciples of Jesus, we have to shape our lives according to his discipline.

The rhythm of Jesus' own life was marked by three movements—quiet prayer, supportive community, and active service—each having a corresponding discipline. As Jesus taught his followers through the rhythm of his own life, he also taught them the disciplines for a life of discipleship. In cultivating a life of quiet prayer, the necessary discipline is trust. In forming a supportive community, the required discipline is forgiveness. And in the life of active service, the essential discipline is compassion. Jesus taught his disciples trust, forgiveness, and compassion through the words and deeds of his own life.

Christian discipline—as the learning that perfects one's discipleship to Jesus—does not have the negative features of command, restraint, and regulation, as is so often assumed today. Living according to Jesus' disciplines creates opportunities in one's life for God to act. The goal of having discipline in one's spiritual life is not to practice restraint and control but to have the freedom to follow Christ more perfectly.

Learning to trust. The Gospels indicate that Jesus made solitary prayer a part of the regular rhythm of his life; and they show Jesus in prayer, particularly at the decisive and critical moments of his life. Through the example of Jesus, we know that in solitary prayer we can learn to trust God. When we are faced with life's critical transitions, we can come to know in quiet that we are God's beloved and can trust that God will guide our spirits because he is with us.

Learning to trust God, and to trust our ability to hear God's voice, does not come easily or automatically. As disciples, we do not directly hear the voice of Jesus giving us clear directives for every decision that faces us. But when we develop the practice of listening prayer, we can gain confidence in our ability to discern and make thoughtful decisions that reflect the movements of God's Spirit and God's will for us. An experienced spiritual director can help us grow in discerning God's guidance.

Sometimes in prayer it is helpful to choose a phrase from the Scriptures for our reflection—a phrase like "Do not be afraid," "The Lord is my shepherd," "You are my beloved," or "Come, follow me." If we keep saying these words and let their truth penetrate our hearts, we will come to believe them and live by them. This is the kind of meditative prayer that establishes trust. By the power of the Spirit, the word of God becomes written on our hearts and becomes the motivation out of which we live our lives.

Jesus listened to the Father's voice throughout his life and walked through his life with confident trust. So whether people approved him or mocked him, praised him or rejected him, or called "Hosanna" or shouted "Crucify," Jesus trusted his Father, knowing that he was chosen and loved. Because of his quiet trust, Jesus didn't feel a personal need to prove anything to others; he didn't have to convince unbelievers in order to settle inner doubts, and he didn't have to compromise to please the crowds. Jesus remained confident in his identity and his mission because he trusted his Father's voice.

When we are unable to trust God, we run around looking for praise, begging for affirmation, and seeking success wherever we can find it. When we learn to trust the Father, as Jesus trusted him, we can be confident disciples who are not anxious, insecure, fearful, or suspicious. With the discipline of trust, born in the silence of prayer, we can deal with both success and failure without losing our sense of identity and trust in God.

Learning to forgive. In each group of people that we experience community with, whether it be a parish, religious order, friendship, family, or marriage, we must forgive one another for not being able to give what only God can give. We need to give and receive forgiveness for our human inability to make one another feel perfectly loved and deeply satisfied. Forgiveness relieves the resentment we feel when we try to get all of our happiness from other people. Forgiveness also relieves the guilt we feel when we fail at our attempts to do for other people what only God can do for them.

The community that Jesus formed was not a club of like-minded individuals. They were a collection of different personalities and temperaments, seeking in their imperfect and faltering ways to be faithful to the mission Jesus gave them. Petty conflicts, wounding words, and hurtful deeds must have been frequent among them. Because Jesus brought together people of differing backgrounds and divergent social and political views, forgiveness within the community of his disciples was imperative.

Jesus told his disciples to forgive seventy times seven times—to forgive endlessly. Forgiveness is the discipline that must be associated with the call to Christian community. Jesus showed the way by forgiving his disciples and even his tormentors. Forgiveness must be the discipline cultivated by all who follow in his way.

Learning compassion. Even before the disciples learned perfectly to listen to God and live together in community, Jesus sent them out to do the work that he did. The discipline most associated with active ministry in the world must be compassion. Learning to look upon the needs of other people with the eyes and heart of Jesus is essential to being his disciples.

Compassion in the Scriptures is, first of all, an attribute of God. The Hebrew word denoting God's compassion is rooted in the word for "womb." God's compassion is a tender, cherishing love. The bond created between God's people by his compassion is like the union between a mother and child or between those who have come from the same womb.

God is described throughout the Old Testament as compassionate in relationship to his people Israel. God's love is never defeated by Israel's unfaithfulness. It always seeks to restore a severed relationship and always longs for union. Divine compassion is more than comforting and tender; it is also creative. God's compassion always brings new birth to a relationship that was threatened or lost.

In Jesus, God's compassion became visible and tangible for us. By entering into our world and becoming one of us, God let us know for sure that he is not a stranger, that he is a compassionate God who is not an outsider. Jesus' response to all those who came to him with their suffering—the hungry, the blind, the widows, the public sinners, and those afflicted by leprosy—flowed from the divine compassion that led God to enter our humanity. Jesus is the embodiment of divine compassion in the world.

The Greek verb used in the Gospels to express the compassionate response of Jesus to those in need is rooted in the word for "entrails" or "bowels." The guts were believed to be the part of the person from which the deepest emotions arise, the center from which both passionate love and passionate hate grow. When the Gospels describe Jesus as "moved with compassion," they are expressing a deep-seated emotion elicited in him by the suffering of others.

Profoundly moved with compassion, Jesus healed those who suffered from leprosy (Mark 1:41), those who were blind (Matthew 20:34), and a boy tormented by a demon (Mark 9:22). Jesus had compassion on hungry crowds (Mark 8:2); he had compassion on a widow and raised her son to life (Luke 7:13); he had compassion on crowds because they were harassed and helpless, like sheep without a shepherd (Mark 6:34). Jesus has walked right into the brokenness of human life and has come to know and experience our afflictions.

Jesus also teaches this compassion in his parables. A father who longed for the return of his runaway son was filled with compassion when he saw his son from afar and ran to embrace him (Luke 15:20). A Samaritan was moved with compassion when he saw an injured man on the side of the road and bandaged his wounds (Luke 10:33). Jesus teaches his followers the discipline of compassion through his own actions and through the lessons of his parables.

The Gospels do not give exclusive focus to the miraculous aspects of Jesus' deeds toward people in need. The fact that sick and tormented people were suddenly released from their pain is wondrous. But what is most important for the writers is the deep, divine compassion that moved Jesus to heal. Jesus is shown to be truly the embodied compassion of God. God's power to heal is inseparable from God's power to feel.

The disciple in active service must imitate Jesus' compassion—the ability to be moved by the pain of another because of the bond we experience with that person. Because we are like children from the same womb, sons and daughters of the same God, we can feel deeply the sufferings of others. Compassion is much different from passing feelings of sorrow or pity. Through cultivating compassion, we take on the eyes and heart of Jesus, and as his disciples we minister his presence in the world.

PETER: THE RECONCILED DISCIPLE

Questions to Begin

10 minutes
Use a question or two to get warmed up for the reading.

1 What is one of the nicknames you have acquired in life?

2 What has been your most drastic role change in life?

Do not scrutinize so closely whether you are doing much or little, ill or well, so long as what you do is not sinful and that you are heartily seeking to do everything for God. Try as far as you can to do everything well, but when it is done, do not think about it. Try, rather, to think of what is to be done next. Go on simply in the Lord's way, and do not torment yourself. We ought to hate our faults, but with a quiet, calm hatred; not pettishly and anxiously.

St. Francis de Sales, *Introduction to the Devout Life*

Opening the Bible

10 minutes
Read the passage aloud. Let individuals take turns reading paragraphs.

The Background

On two separate occasions Peter received the call "Follow me." These were the first and last words Jesus spoke to him (Mark 1:17; John 21:19). A whole training in discipleship lay between these two calls. The first occasion was at the Sea of Galilee, when Peter left his fishing nets and joined Jesus on the great adventure of fishing for people. The second occasion was when the risen Lord encountered Peter again at the Sea of Galilee. This time Jesus called Peter to care for his flock. Both times, Jesus offered Peter the grace he needed for following him. Our readings portray Peter at his worst and at his best: his denial of Jesus during Jesus' trial, and his later affirmation of his love for Jesus.

The Reading: John 18:1–13, 15–19, 25–27; 21:1–19

Peter at the Arrest of Jesus

18:1 Jesus . . . went out with his disciples across the Kidron valley to a place where there was a garden, which he and his disciples entered. 2 Now Judas, who betrayed him, also knew the place, because Jesus often met there with his disciples. 3 So Judas brought a detachment of soldiers together with police from the chief priests and the Pharisees, and they came there with lanterns and torches and weapons. 4 Then Jesus, knowing all that was to happen to him, came forward and asked them, "Whom are you looking for?" 5 They answered, "Jesus of Nazareth." Jesus replied, "I am he." Judas, who betrayed him, was standing with them. 6 When Jesus said to them, "I am he," they stepped back and fell to the ground. 7 Again he asked them, "Whom are you looking for?" And they said, "Jesus of Nazareth." 8 Jesus answered, "I told you that I am he. So if you are looking for me, let these men go." 9 This was to fulfill the word that he had spoken, "I did not lose a single one of those whom you gave me." 10 Then Simon Peter, who had a sword, drew it, struck the high priest's slave, and cut off his right ear. The slave's name was Malchus. 11 Jesus said to Peter, "Put your sword back into its sheath. Am I not to drink the cup that the Father has given me?"

12 So the soldiers, their officer, and the Jewish police arrested Jesus and bound him. 13 First they took him to Annas, who was the father-in-law of Caiaphas, the high priest that year. . . .

15 Simon Peter and another disciple followed Jesus. Since that disciple was known to the high priest, he went with Jesus into the courtyard of the high priest, 16 but Peter was standing outside at the gate. So the other disciple, who was known to the high priest, went out, spoke to the woman who guarded the gate, and brought Peter in. 17 The woman said to Peter, "You are not also one of this man's disciples, are you?" He said, "I am not." 18 Now the slaves and the police had made a charcoal fire because it was cold, and they were standing around it and warming themselves. Peter also was standing with them and warming himself.

19 Then the high priest questioned Jesus about his disciples and about his teaching. . . .

25 Now Simon Peter was standing and warming himself. They asked him, "You are not also one of his disciples, are you?" He denied it and said, "I am not." 26 One of the slaves of the high priest, a relative of the man whose ear Peter had cut off, asked, "Did I not see you in the garden with him?" 27 Again Peter denied it, and at that moment the cock crowed.

Jesus Calls Peter to Shepherd His Flock

21:1 After these things Jesus showed himself again to the disciples by the Sea of Tiberias; and he showed himself in this way. 2 Gathered there together were Simon Peter, Thomas called the Twin, Nathanael of Cana in Galilee, the sons of Zebedee, and two others of his disciples. 3 Simon Peter said to them, "I am going fishing." They said to him, "We will go with you." They went out and got into the boat, but that night they caught nothing.

4 Just after daybreak, Jesus stood on the beach; but the disciples did not know that it was Jesus. 5 Jesus said to them, "Children, you have no fish, have you?" They answered him, "No." 6 He said to them, "Cast the net to the right side of the boat, and you will find some." So they cast it, and now they were not able to haul it in because there were so many fish. 7 That disciple whom Jesus loved said to Peter, "It is the Lord!" When Simon Peter heard that it

was the Lord, he put on some clothes, for he was naked, and jumped into the sea. 8 But the other disciples came in the boat, dragging the net full of fish, for they were not far from the land, only about a hundred yards off.

9 When they had gone ashore, they saw a charcoal fire there, with fish on it, and bread. 10 Jesus said to them, "Bring some of the fish that you have just caught." 11 So Simon Peter went aboard and hauled the net ashore, full of large fish, a hundred fifty-three of them; and though there were so many, the net was not torn. 12 Jesus said to them, "Come and have breakfast." Now none of the disciples dared to ask him, "Who are you?" because they knew it was the Lord. 13 Jesus came and took the bread and gave it to them, and did the same with the fish. 14 This was now the third time that Jesus appeared to the disciples after he was raised from the dead.

15 When they had finished breakfast, Jesus said to Simon Peter, "Simon son of John, do you love me more than these?" He said to him, "Yes, Lord; you know that I love you." Jesus said to him, "Feed my lambs." 16 A second time he said to him, "Simon son of John, do you love me?" He said to him, "Yes, Lord; you know that I love you." Jesus said to him, "Tend my sheep." 17 He said to him the third time, "Simon son of John, do you love me?" Peter felt hurt because he said to him the third time, "Do you love me?" And he said to him, "Lord, you know everything; you know that I love you." Jesus said to him, "Feed my sheep. 18 Very truly, I tell you, when you were younger, you used to fasten your own belt and to go wherever you wished. But when you grow old, you will stretch out your hands, and someone else will fasten a belt around you and take you where you do not wish to go." 19 (He said this to indicate the kind of death by which he would glorify God.) After this he said to him, "Follow me."

First Impression

5 minutes
Briefly mention a question you have about the reading or one thing in it that surprised, impressed, delighted, or challenged you. No discussion! Just listen to one another's reactions.

Exploring the Theme

If participants have not read this section already, read it aloud. Otherwise go on to "Questions for Reflection and Discussion."

To study the life of Peter in the Gospels is to experience a deep lesson in knowing and following Jesus. Peter (then called Simon) was the first disciple called by Jesus to follow him (Mark 1:16–17), and he is always the first person named on the lists of the Twelve (Mark 3:16). He is often the spokesperson for the others (Mark 8:29), and in Matthew's Gospel he is named by Jesus as the "rock" on which Jesus will build his church (Matthew 16:18).

Yet surprisingly, the Gospel writers do not hesitate to show us the negative side of Peter. He is impulsive, he misunderstands Jesus, his faith is shaky, and he even denies Jesus in his time of crisis. Nevertheless, Peter became a great model for discipleship because he learned from his failures and accepted the forgiveness that Jesus offered him.

18:1–27. In this scene of Jesus' arrest, Peter exemplifies the breakdown of discipleship. Jesus, who has come "as light into the world," calls his followers into the light so that they do not "remain in the darkness" (12:46). The drama of the account revolves around whether Peter, who has been called into the light by Jesus, will remain in the light or fall back into the darkness.

The suffering of Jesus begins at night in a garden where Jesus often met with his disciples (18:2). Judas brings the forces of darkness to this place. They are carrying their own sources of light—lanterns and torches—searching for "the light of the world" (8:12; 9:5). Judas is "standing with them" (18:5) on the side of the darkness. In the dramatic confrontation, Jesus' own luminous, divine nature shines through and overwhelms those seeking to destroy him (18:6). His concern is for his disciples, and he offers himself in place of them, so that not a single one is lost to the darkness (18:8–9).

The violent power used by those who have come with weapons in the darkness (18:3) forms a strong contrast with the liberating power to be demonstrated in Christ's own death and resurrection. Succumbing to fear, Peter draws his sword and cuts off an ear of the high priest's slave (18:10). Peter's violent attempt to change the course of events would thwart God's designs.

Peter and "another disciple" follow Jesus to the courtyard of the high priest (18:15). Yet Peter loses his nerve when identified by the servants as one of Jesus' disciples. While Jesus courageously proclaims his identity and mission before the high priest (18:19–24), Peter crumples in fear and denies his discipleship (18:17, 25). Here, like Judas, Peter is "also standing with them" (18:18) on the side of the darkness. Having denied the one who is the light of the world, he warms himself in the night at a paltry source of light, the charcoal fire.

The cock crow is Peter's harsh awaking to his failure. That haunting signal in the night brings us back to the words of Jesus at the Last Supper. There, Peter had insisted on his unswerving loyalty to Jesus: "I will lay down my life for you." Jesus responded to Peter's brave promise with these prophetic words: "Very truly, I tell you, before the cock crows, you will have denied me three times" (13:37–38).

Peter's failure is not overcome during the dark scenes of Christ's crucifixion and death. Jesus had told him at the Last Supper, "Where I am going, you cannot follow me now; but you will follow me afterward" (13:36). Only in the light of Jesus' resurrection will Peter be reconciled with his master and follow him once again.

21:1–14. Back near the Sea of Galilee—here called the Sea of Tiberias—where Jesus had called his first disciples, his disciples fish all night in the darkness but catch nothing (21:3). But in the light of daybreak, the risen Jesus stands before them. He orders them to cast their nets, and they bring in an enormous catch (21:6).

Fishing represents the mission of discipleship, as we saw in Peter's call to fish for people (Mark 1:17). In the darkness, the mission is unsuccessful; in the light of Christ, the results are massive. Based on the ancient commentary of St. Jerome, which holds that there were 153 known varieties of fish at the time, the great catch that Peter brings to shore represents the mission of the disciples to all the nations of the world (21:11). It is the symbolic equivalent of the great commission that Jesus gives his followers at the end of Matthew's Gospel: "Go therefore and make disciples of all nations" (Matthew 28:19).

The charcoal fire (21:9) must remind Peter of the charcoal fire outside the high priest's house (18:18). How different this fire looks in the light of dawn with the nourishing bread and fish grilling upon it! The remembered scene of fear and denial is replaced by a meal of Reconciliation and Communion prepared by the risen Lord.

21:15–19. As Jesus questions Peter three times about his love for him, he provides Peter with the opportunity to reverse his threefold denial made during that awful night in the courtyard of the high priest. Jesus' persistent questioning is difficult for Peter, who feels hurt when Jesus asks him the same question for the third time (21:17). Yet Peter must accept this humbling experience and be prepared to prove his commitment and trustworthiness after his previous infidelity.

As the shepherd of God's flock, Peter must care for the sheep according to the loving and sacrificial example of Jesus. Jesus knows that Peter will be asked to offer the ultimate witness to love by giving up his life in martyrdom (21:19), and Jesus seems confident that Peter will remain faithful to the end. Jesus' "Follow me," the call first given to Peter on these same shores, is now a call to a matured discipleship, a discipleship that has been tempered and enriched by failure and forgiveness.

Reflections. Experience has shown that those who are forgiven the most are able to love the most. Stripped of his pride and self-reliance, Peter was able to say "I love you" with a self-sacrificing love and to become what Jesus called him to be—the great rock, the fisherman, and the shepherd of the Church.

Questions for Reflection and Discussion

45 minutes
Choose questions according to your interest and time.

1 What do you think was going through Peter's mind as he stood warming himself by the charcoal fire (18:18)?

2 Why do you think John included the account of Peter's three denials? Would it not have been better to omit the failure of the church's most visible leader?

3 What did Peter deny about Jesus when questioned in the courtyard of the high priest? What did Peter deny about himself? In what ways do you—directly or indirectly—deny the truth about yourself?

4 How has your courage as a disciple been tested? What could you do to become a more committed disciple of Jesus?

5 How do you think Peter felt when he saw the charcoal fire that Jesus had prepared on the shore (21:9)?

6 Why do you think the risen Jesus used the scene of the great catch to symbolize Peter's role as fisher of people?

7   How do you suppose Peter
     felt by the end of Jesus' third
     question, "Do you love me?"
     (21:17)? How would you have
     felt?

8   Why is it difficult to earn the
     trust of loved ones after a
     betrayal? What are the most
     effective steps?

9   For personal reflection: Who
     do you know who needs to feel
     forgiven by you today? What can
     you do to offer forgiveness?

10   **Focus question.** What can
     Peter's experiences teach you
     about being a disciple of Jesus?
     How can you apply what you
     have learned about Peter to your
     own life?

10 minutes
Use this approach—or create your own!

♦ Give the participants a few moments to silently recall times in which they have denied Christ and denied their own discipleship. Then slowly pray the following prayer for forgiveness together.

Leader: As God's family, with confidence let us ask the Father's forgiveness, for he is full of gentleness and compassion.

All: I confess to Almighty God,
And to you, my brothers and sisters,
That I have sinned through my own fault
In my thoughts and in my words,
In what I have done, and in what I have failed to do;
And I ask Blessed Mary, ever virgin,
All the angels and saints,
And you, my brothers and sisters,
To pray for me to the Lord our God.

Leader: May almighty God have mercy on us, forgive us our sins, and bring us to everlasting life.

All: Amen.

Between Discussions

The Minor Gospel Characters as Model Disciples

Throughout each of the four Gospels, the portrayal of the chosen disciples of Jesus is remarkably candid. The gospel writers seem to pay special attention to the weaknesses and failures of the disciples. While they are still in Galilee, the chosen disciples are consistently slow to grasp the teachings of Jesus: they do not fully understand who he is, they protest his teachings about the cross, they are fearful in the midst of a storm on the sea. But it is in Jerusalem that their discipleship is most severely tested. The disciples self-righteously object to a woman who anoints Jesus. One of them goes to barter for Jesus' betrayal. At the Last Supper, Jesus predicts treachery by Judas and desertion and denial by the rest of the disciples. During his agony in the garden, his closest disciples cannot stay awake with him. When the enemies of Jesus come for his arrest, his disciples prove cowardly. One of them retaliates with the violence of a sword, showing a total lack of understanding of Jesus and his mission. All of them abandon Jesus and flee in panic. Peter follows at a distance, but his fears soon overwhelm him as he vehemently denies his discipleship at the moment when Jesus is put on trial. As Jesus is crucified, those whom we would have expected to be near him at the cross have all fled in fear.

It is often the people who play a smaller role in the Gospel accounts—those sometimes called "minor" characters—who exemplify authentic disciples. The public sinners, outcasts, and seemingly unimportant people are consistently shown to be more open to the message Jesus taught than the righteous are. A tax collector, a prostitute, a blind man, a foreign woman, a poor widow—these unexpected characters often have more to teach the reader about how to follow Jesus than the disciples with more prominent roles. Let us look at some of these minor characters who teach us major lessons about how best to follow Jesus. (The following comments will make the most sense if you also read the Gospel passages).

The woman who anointed Jesus (Mark 14:3–9). The account of this woman at Bethany stands out like an oasis in the midst of treachery and betrayal. Her act of extravagant generosity in anointing Jesus with costly perfumed oil is a foreshadowing of the unreserved and total love that Jesus will demonstrate in his passion. Notice that the woman did not open the jar and carefully measure out an appropriate amount. Rather, she broke open the jar so that its entire contents were lavishly poured out upon Jesus. Despite the protests of the observers, Jesus vigorously defended and praised the action of this woman as an example of authentic discipleship. He said, "Wherever the good news is proclaimed in the whole world, what she has done will be told in remembrance of her." Her act of love was generous, lavish, and total—a gift of her whole self to the one who was giving his life for her.

Simon of Cyrene, who carried the cross (Mark 15:21). Simon was a Jewish man who had arrived from Cyrene in northern Africa, possibly fulfilling a life's ambition to come to Jerusalem for the pilgrimage feast of Passover. He happened to be passing by when the soldiers were leading the condemned Jesus out of the city gates. The soldiers coerced Simon into his role of taking up the crossbeam of Jesus' cross, probably because Jesus was so physically weak from his torturous flogging. What must have seemed to Simon at first a terrible indignity—carrying the cross of a condemned man—became his moment of glory. Jesus had taught that whoever wanted to be his disciple must take up the cross. The image of Simon carrying the cross of Jesus stands forever as an image of true discipleship at a moment when all the chosen disciples of Jesus had fled.

The criminal who was crucified with Jesus (Luke 23:32–33, 39–43). Two condemned criminals are crucified with Jesus, "one on his right and one on his left." Their words reveal two radically different responses to Jesus. The unrepentant criminal joins in the mockery, challenging Jesus to save himself. But the other criminal demonstrates a two-step process of conversion. First, he acknowledges his sins, then he turns to Jesus for help: "Jesus, remember me when you come into your kingdom." Throughout his life Jesus has had a particular bond with public sinners and outcasts. Now he is put to death with these kinds of companions. His response to the dying criminal expresses the gift of immediate salvation: "Truly I tell you, today you will be with me in Paradise." Jesus, the one who came "to seek out and save the lost," continued to welcome the outcast and the sinner until his final breath.

The Roman centurion professing faith in Jesus

(Mark 15:39). In the Roman army, the centurion was the commander of a company of soldiers and the army's backbone. Though this centurion at the cross is not named in the Gospels, later tradition gave him the name Longinus and honored him as a Christian saint. Presumably, this man was in charge of Jesus' crucifixion and its details: the walk to Golgotha, the division of his clothing, and the nailing to the cross between two criminals. The awful Crucifixion and death became divine revelation for this gentile centurion, and he professed faith in Jesus: "Now when the centurion, who stood facing him, saw that in this way he breathed his last, he said, 'Truly this man was God's Son!'" The centurion's words are the climactic expression of Christian belief in Mark's Gospel, and his profession of faith foreshadows the vast multitudes from throughout the Roman Empire who will come to believe in Jesus.

The women of Galilee who remained with Jesus

(Mark 15:40–41). Many women who were followers of Jesus from his ministry in Galilee were "looking on from a distance" during his crucifixion and death. Though at a safe distance, these women were close enough to be sympathetic witnesses to these climactic events. Their presence during Jesus' dark hours is a stark reminder of the chosen twelve's flight and absence at the cross. Among these "many women," the Gospels mention a few by name. Mary Magdalene is the first named in each listing of the Galilean female followers. In addition, Mark names Salome and another Mary. Matthew adds the mother of the sons of Zebedee. John adds the mother of Jesus.

The terms used to describe these Galilean women are words that refer to faithful discipleship. They "followed Jesus" through Galilee and on his journey to Jerusalem; they "provided for him," a term referring to their service of Jesus in ministering to the needs of his mission; and they "had come up with him to Jerusalem," words referring to their unity with him in the way of suffering and the fulfillment of his mission at the cross. These women also watched as Jesus was laid in the tomb, and they sat facing the tomb in silent vigil. They would be the first to discover the empty tomb and to encounter the risen Christ. They are the consistent witnesses through the Galilean ministry, to the cross, to the tomb, and to the Resurrection. Their faithful following and service is a model for all future disciples.

Joseph of Arimathea, who laid the body of Jesus in the tomb (Mark 15:42–46). Joseph was a respected member of the Jewish council in Jerusalem—the Sanhedrin—the very body that had handed Jesus over to the Romans to be executed. His relationship to Jesus during his lifetime is unclear in the Gospels: Mark tells us that he was "waiting expectantly for the kingdom of God," meaning that he was open and responsive to the message of Jesus. Matthew and John call him a "disciple" of Jesus, but John notes that he was a "secret" disciple out of fear of the Jewish leaders. But somehow the suffering of Jesus stirred Joseph's heart and removed his fears. According to Jewish law, a body could not be left on the cross overnight. The law also forbade burial after the Sabbath began. So Joseph went to Pilate at sundown and petitioned for the body of Jesus so that he could give it an immediate burial.

It must have been a profoundly mysterious experience to take down the lifeless body of Jesus from the cross, tenderly wrap it in a linen cloth, and carry it to its rocky tomb. Joseph laid his body on the prepared slab within the tomb and rolled the heavy stone into its groove against the tomb's door. The boldness of Joseph of Arimathea in publicly identifying himself with Jesus after his death is a strong contrast to the cowardly disciples, who fled from Jesus in his final hours. Joseph did what the chosen disciples of Jesus should have done.

JOHN: THE BELOVED DISCIPLE

Questions to Begin

10 minutes
Use a question or two to get warmed up for the reading.

1 Think of one of your oldest and dearest friends. What do you appreciate most about this kind of friendship?

2 When have you wanted to remain anonymous?

From the beginning, Jesus associated his disciples with his own life, revealed the mystery of the Kingdom to them, and he gave them a share in his mission, joy, and sufferings. Jesus spoke of a still more intimate communion between him and those who would follow him: "Abide in me, and I in you. . . . I am the vine, you are the branches." And he proclaimed a mysterious and real communion between his own body and ours: "He who eats my flesh and drinks my blood abides in me, and I in him."

Catechism of the Catholic Church, section 787

Opening the Bible

10 minutes
*Read the passage aloud. Let individuals take turns reading
paragraphs.*

The Background

In several places throughout the Gospel of John, the writer refers to
an unnamed disciple who had a particularly close relationship with
Jesus. This disciple is referred to as the "beloved disciple" or the
"disciple whom Jesus loved." At the end of the Gospel, this disciple
is designated as the one who wrote the Gospel and testified to the
truth of the Gospel's tradition about Jesus (John 21:24). The fourth
Gospel, like the other three Gospels, was written anonymously
and here the author clearly intends to remain anonymous. The
designation "according to John" was not appended to the Gospel
until the second century. From the second century until recent
times, most Christians have concluded that the author was one of
the Twelve—namely, John, the son of Zebedee. While there is much
to recommend this conclusion, it is far from certain. In any case,
what we find in this Gospel is a unique expression of the good news
of Jesus, which has few precise parallels with the other Gospels. A
study of this "beloved disciple" will help us better understand the
purpose and message of this intriguing Gospel.

The Reading: John 13:21–30; 19:25–27, 31–35; 20:3–10; 21:4–8, 20–24

The Beloved Disciple Reclines next to Jesus at the Last Supper

13:21 After saying this Jesus was troubled in spirit, and declared,
"Very truly, I tell you, one of you will betray me." 22 The disciples
looked at one another, uncertain of whom he was speaking. 23 One
of his disciples—the one whom Jesus loved—was reclining next
to him; 24 Simon Peter therefore motioned to him to ask Jesus of
whom he was speaking. 25 So while reclining next to Jesus, he asked
him, "Lord, who is it?" 26 Jesus answered, "It is the one to whom I
give this piece of bread when I have dipped it in the dish." So when
he had dipped the piece of bread, he gave it to Judas son of Simon
Iscariot. 27 After he received the piece of bread, Satan entered into
him. Jesus said to him, "Do quickly what you are going to do."

28 Now no one at the table knew why he said this to him. 29 Some thought that, because Judas had the common purse, Jesus was telling him, "Buy what we need for the festival"; or, that he should give something to the poor. 30 So, after receiving the piece of bread, he immediately went out. And it was night.

The Crucified Jesus Entrusts His Mother to the Beloved Disciple

19:25 Meanwhile, standing near the cross of Jesus were his mother, and his mother's sister, Mary the wife of Clopas, and Mary Magdalene. 26 When Jesus saw his mother and the disciple whom he loved standing beside her, he said to his mother, "Woman, here is your son." 27 Then he said to the disciple, "Here is your mother." And from that hour the disciple took her into his own home.

The Disciple Witnesses Christ's Death

19:31 Since it was the day of Preparation, the Jews did not want the bodies left on the cross during the sabbath, especially because that sabbath was a day of great solemnity. So they asked Pilate to have the legs of the crucified men broken and the bodies removed. 32 Then the soldiers came and broke the legs of the first and of the other who had been crucified with him. 33 But when they came to Jesus and saw that he was already dead, they did not break his legs. 34 Instead, one of the soldiers pierced his side with a spear, and at once blood and water came out. 35 (He who saw this has testified so that you also may believe. His testimony is true, and he knows that he tells the truth.)

The Disciple and Peter Race to Jesus' Tomb

20:3 Then Peter and the other disciple set out and went toward the tomb. 4 The two were running together, but the other disciple outran Peter and reached the tomb first. 5 He bent down to look in and saw the linen wrappings lying there, but he did not go in. 6 Then Simon Peter came, following him, and went into the tomb. He saw the linen wrappings lying there, 7 and the cloth that had been on Jesus' head, not lying with the linen wrappings but rolled up in a place by itself. 8 Then the other disciple, who reached the tomb first, also went in, and he saw and believed; [9] for as yet they did not understand the scripture, that he must rise from the dead. [10] Then the disciples returned to their homes.

The Disciple Recognizes the Risen Lord

21:4 Just after daybreak, Jesus stood on the beach; but the disciples did not know that it was Jesus. [5] Jesus said to them, "Children, you have no fish, have you?" They answered him, "No." [6] He said to them, "Cast the net to the right side of the boat, and you will find some." So they cast it, and now they were not able to haul it in because there were so many fish. [7] That disciple whom Jesus loved said to Peter, "It is the Lord!" When Simon Peter heard that it was the Lord, he put on some clothes, for he was naked, and jumped into the sea. [8] But the other disciples came in the boat, dragging the net full of fish, for they were not far from the land, only about a hundred yards off.

The Beloved Disciple Is Identified as the Gospel Writer

21:20 Peter turned and saw the disciple whom Jesus loved following them; he was the one who had reclined next to Jesus at the supper and had said, "Lord, who is it that is going to betray you?" [21] When Peter saw him, he said to Jesus, "Lord, what about him?" [22] Jesus said to him, "If it is my will that he remain until I come, what is that to you? Follow me!" [23] So the rumor spread in the community that this disciple would not die. Yet Jesus did not say to him that he would not die, but, "If it is my will that he remain until I come, what is that to you?" [24] This is the disciple who is testifying to these things and has written them, and we know that his testimony is true.

First Impression

5 minutes
Briefly mention a question you have about the reading or one thing in it that surprised, impressed, delighted, or challenged you. No discussion! Just listen to one another's reactions.

Exploring the Theme

If participants have not read this section already, read it aloud. Otherwise go on to "Questions for Reflection and Discussion."

13:21–30. This solemn and disturbing moment for Jesus and his disciples takes place within the intimacy of table fellowship. Jesus is anguished in his depths and announces that one of his disciples will betray him. The revelation comes as a shock to the disciples, who want to know who the betrayer could be. At this critical point in the Gospel, "the beloved disciple" is introduced, a character who is never identified by name. This "one whom Jesus loved" is said to be "reclining next to" Jesus (13:23). His position at the table was regarded by the disciples as a place of special honor. The reclining posture was characteristic of formal meals and was the required posture for the Jewish Passover meal. The word for "next to" is the same Greek word used in the Gospel's prologue stating that the Son is "close to" the Father's heart (1:18). The disciple's position close to the heart of Jesus is a symbol of the disciple's affection and commitment.

Asked by Simon Peter to find out the traitor's identity, the beloved disciple asks Jesus, "Lord, who is it?" Jesus then tells the disciple that he will share an intimate gesture with the betrayer: dipping the morsel into the dish and sharing it with him. This final gesture of love by Jesus to his disloyal disciple is definitely rejected, and Judas goes out into the darkness. Because Jesus had revealed the meaning of his gesture only to the beloved disciple, it seems that only this disciple understands the significance of Jesus' gesture and of Judas's departure.

19:25–27. Lifted up on the cross, Jesus joins his mother and his beloved disciple together. To his mother, he says, "Here is your son"; to the disciple, "Here is your mother." Given the rich symbolism of John's Gospel and the climactic nature of this moment in Jesus' life, Jesus cannot simply mean that he wishes the disciple to look after his mother after his death. By these words, Jesus makes his mother the mother of all future disciples; all disciples become her children. The disciple Jesus loved and Mary, the mother he loved, represent the new family of God—his Church—created at the Crucifixion.

19:31–35. Not only does Jesus form his Church at the cross, but at his death he pours out all the means of the Church's life. In his focus on the water and blood that flow from Jesus' body, the author hints at the "water" of Baptism (3:5; 7:37–39) and the "blood" of the Eucharist (6:53–56)—the ongoing sources of Jesus' life in his disciples in every age. From the side of the pierced savior flows the life of his Church.

Here the author—or perhaps the later editor—launches into a personal comment that is unparallel to the rest of the Gospel. The witness to this scene is evidently the beloved disciple, the one who "has testified" so that the readers of the Gospel may believe (19:35). It is his testimony that is the source of truth and credibility for the Gospel. He has communicated the revelation of the Son to the world, and he shows that this revelation continues in the flowing water and spilled blood of Baptism and the Eucharist in Christ's Church.

20:3–10. In the dawning light of Easter morning, the beloved disciple and Simon Peter race to the tomb. The beloved one has the edge on Peter both in speed and insight. Though the beloved disciple reaches the tomb first, he steps aside to allow Peter to enter the tomb ahead of him. What Peter sees is carefully described, but his reaction is not. Yet when the other disciple enters the tomb, we are told, "he saw and believed" (20:8). Like the Christians of the community who received his gospel, the beloved disciple believed in Jesus' resurrection on the evidence that God provided, not by seeing the risen Lord. What he observed was that Jesus was not in the tomb. The earliest readers of the Gospel would have the beloved disciple's testimony as well as a more developed understanding of "the scripture, that he must rise from the dead." Witness and word would be the foundation for their Easter faith. The beloved disciple's faith is the model for all the readers of his Gospel: "Blessed are those who have not seen and yet have come to believe" (20:29).

21:4–8. The early morning scene at the Sea of Tiberias involved seven disciples, two of whom remain anonymous (21:2). Following the remarkable catch of fish, "that disciple whom Jesus loved" recognized the risen Lord (21:7). He said to Peter, "It is the Lord!" The revelation of the beloved disciple brought an energetic response from Peter, who jumped into the lake while the others hauled ashore the boat filled with fish.

21:20–24. The final words of the Gospel are about the beloved disciple. Once again, he is described alongside Peter. The paths of these two disciples have been entwined across the last scenes of the Gospel, from the Last Supper to the empty tomb. In contrast to Peter's early death by martyrdom, the beloved disciple is to live out a long life of faithful love. Jesus indicates that both forms of discipleship are equally valid.

The beloved disciple must have been one of the last of the original disciples to die. His imminent death may have been the occasion for writing these final words of the Gospel. They are meant to clarify the words of Jesus about the destiny of the disciple he loved. Jesus did not say that the beloved disciple would not die; he said, rather, that the disciple's future would be determined by the will of Jesus.

The beloved disciple is the Gospel's eyewitness to the life of Jesus and the story's anonymous narrator (21:24). It is not necessary that the beloved disciple has written every word himself to be called the author. He is the author because he is the principal source of what was handed on in the writings. Clearly the final verses were written by someone else, vouching for the beloved disciple's trustworthiness: "We know that his testimony is true." This testimony, the editor admits, is only a small part of the entire life of Jesus: "But there are also many other things that Jesus did; if every one of them were written down, I suppose that the world itself could not contain the books that would be written" (21:25).

Reflections. Living out Jesus' call to "follow me" was different for every disciple. For Peter, following meant imitating Jesus as the shepherd and meeting a violent death similar to Jesus'. For the beloved disciple, following meant something quite different. His discipleship meant living a long life, testifying and witnessing to the life of Jesus, and remaining close to the heart of Jesus.

Questions for Reflection and Discussion

45 minutes
Choose questions according to your interest and time.

1 Is it shocking that the betrayer of Jesus is revealed in the context of a meal with his disciples? What do you suppose the disciples were feeling?

2 The beloved disciple's belief in the resurrection of Jesus is described in two scenes: one at the empty tomb and the other at the sea. Contrast the ways that he came to believe in these scenes. What helps you to recognize the Lord's presence?

3 Contrast the models of discipleship represented by Peter and the beloved disciple. What significance do the similarities and the differences have for your understanding of discipleship?

4 Jesus established his new family at the cross by joining the lives of his mother and his beloved disciple. In what ways have you welcomed Mary into your life?

5 At his death, Jesus gave his Church the means to sustain its life. How do Jesus' "blood" and "water" sustain your life? What would your life be like without them?

6 How do you know when a person's testimony is true? What is the most important evidence for your belief in Christ's resurrection?

7 **Focus question.** What is unique about the discipleship of the beloved disciple? What aspects of his discipleship would you most like to imitate? How can you apply what you have learned about the beloved disciple to your own life?

Prayer to Close

10 minutes
Use this approach—or create your own!

♦ Ask a participant to read 1 John 5:6–12 aloud. Then pray these prayers of thanksgiving together:

Leader: For the gift of the Spirit, who testifies to the truth . . .
Response: We thank you, God of Life.

Leader: For the waters of baptism, which bring us into the family of God . . .
Response: We thank you, God of Life.

Leader: For the saving blood of Christ, which redeems us from sin and death . . .
Response: We thank you, God of Life.

Allow group members to add their own prayers of thanksgiving.

Between Discussions

Who Is the Mysterious "Beloved Disciple"?

The author of the Gospel of John makes it clear that the source of the testimony about Jesus is an unnamed disciple referred to as "that disciple whom Jesus loved" (John 21:7). According to an ancient tradition, this beloved disciple is John, son of Zebedee, one of the Twelve—a tradition reflected in the fact that this Gospel is called "the Gospel of John." How did the beloved disciple come to be identified as John?

The reasoning begins with the fact that Jesus had an inner circle of followers. In the Gospels of Matthew, Mark, and Luke, the first disciples called by Jesus are Peter and Andrew, followed by James and John—the sons of Zebedee. Throughout these Gospels, James and John are almost always seen together. Along with Peter, they form a kind of inner circle present with Jesus, as on the Mount of Transfiguration and in the Garden of Gethsemane.

It seems that the beloved disciple must have been one of Jesus' inner circle since he is so frequently associated with Peter (John 13:24; 18:15–16; 20:2–3) and because he reclined next to Jesus (John 13:23) at the supper. Which of the inner four might the beloved disciple have been? Clearly the beloved disciple is not Peter. Nor is he Andrew, for Andrew is mentioned by name several times in the Gospel of John. This leaves James and John, who are never named in the Gospel of John. Their bold request in the other Gospels, to sit on the right and left of Jesus in his glory, may indicate that those were already their customary places in their earthly meals with Jesus. If the choice is between James and John, we can safely rule out James because his early death (Acts 12:2) left him little time to have written a Gospel. Thus, through a process of elimination, we are led to Zebedee's other son, the apostle John.

In addition to this evidence from the four Gospels, the Acts of the Apostles connects the ministry of Peter and John in the early Church. After the ascension of Jesus, John is seen with Peter in Jerusalem at the Beautiful Gate of the temple (Acts 3:1–11) and before the ruling council, or Sanhedrin (Acts 4:1–23). Later, Peter and John are sent together by the church in Jerusalem to Samaria to confer the Holy Spirit on those who had come to believe there (Acts 8:14–25). When the accounts of Peter and the beloved disciple in John's Gospel are placed beside the accounts of Peter and John in

Acts, they read as if one were simply a continuation of the other. If the early Christians read these books together, the identification of the beloved disciple as John the apostle seems an easy step to take.

For these reasons, the idea that the beloved disciple is John the apostle is found almost universally in the Christian tradition—beginning in the second century. Further evidence is that Irenaeus and several other early writers link the apostle John to the church in Ephesus (in today's western Turkey), and Ephesus is the most likely site for the composition of the Gospel of John. In fact, Irenaeus states explicitly that "John, the disciple of the Lord, who also had leaned upon his breast, did himself publish a gospel during his residence at Ephesus." Irenaeus also wrote that John remained among the community of believers in Ephesus until the reign of the emperor Trajan, who ruled from AD 98 to 117, and then died there.

Although the identification of the beloved disciple as John the apostle is well attested in Christian history and art, the evidence makes it far from certain. Many scholars today agree that evidence within the fourth Gospel makes it difficult to substantiate this claim.

Two other references to an anonymous disciple, besides the ones we have discussed, occur toward the beginning and the end of John's Gospel. Near the beginning of this Gospel, we see John the Baptist standing at Bethany across the Jordan with two of his disciples (1:28, 35). As Jesus walks by, John the Baptist points him out as the Lamb of God. The two disciples hear John the Baptist, and they begin to follow Jesus (1:36–39). One of these disciples is Andrew; the other is unnamed. We may presume that this anonymous disciple is the same "other disciple" described later in the Gospel as "the one Jesus loved." The other reference to an anonymous disciple in John's Gospel occurs shortly after the arrest of Jesus. When Jesus is brought to the house of the high priest, Peter and "another disciple" follow. They are able to enter the courtyard of the high priest because the other disciple was "known to the high priest" (18:15–16). Again, this anonymous disciple seems to be the same as "the one Jesus loved." Because this anonymous disciple was a former disciple of John the Baptist and had some connection to the high priest at the temple, this disciple was more likely a man from Judea in the south rather than a Galilean.

Another credible opinion holds that the beloved disciple is Lazarus. In the account of the climactic miracle of the Gospel, Jesus went to the tomb of Lazarus and began to weep (11:35). This caused the bystanders to comment, "See how he loved him!" (11:36). Since Lazarus lived in Bethany, a village near Jerusalem, he could have more easily been a former disciple of John the Baptist as well as "known to the high priest" (18:15). It may be significant that Lazarus's sisters, when speaking to Jesus, refer to their brother as "he whom you love" (John 11:3; compare also 11:36).

It is clear that the author of John 21 does not identify the beloved disciple with John, the son of Zebedee. In the final Resurrection narrative of the Gospel, the author states that seven disciples of Jesus were gathered at the Sea of Galilee: Peter, Thomas, Nathanael, the sons of Zebedee, and two other disciples. The sons of Zebedee (James and John) are mentioned separately from two later references to "the disciple whom Jesus loved," the one who recognized the risen Lord (21:7, 20).

Modern historians point out that many people in the second-century Church were suspicious of the fourth Gospel because it was so different from the other Gospels and because it was so popular among some heretical groups. Those who supported its inclusion in the Christian canon, among whom Irenaeus was the foremost, were eager to demonstrate the Gospel's apostolic origins. If it could be shown to have originated with an apostle, then the Gospel could be accepted by orthodox Christians. This led Irenaeus to support the tradition that circulated around Ephesus at the time to the effect that the Gospel was written by John, the beloved disciple of the Lord. Historians speculate that Irenaeus might not have been in a position to actually verify this tradition.

A final reason for skepticism about the authorship of the fourth Gospel by John the apostle is offered by biblical scholars who study the Gospel's text. Its language, its highly developed symbolism, and its theological understanding of Christ go well beyond what many scholars think would have been likely for a fisherman from Galilee.

So the possibility remains that Jesus had other disciples in addition to the Twelve—disciples who came from around Jerusalem rather than Galilee—and that the beloved disciple was one of these. Many scholars today prefer to respect the disciple's anonymity and make no precise identification.

Despite the many arguments for or against identifying the beloved disciple as John or some other figure in the early Christian community, one fact remains that we must remember: this Gospel is anonymous by the author's choice and design. While keeping this fact in mind, let me propose a partial answer to the mystery of the identity of the beloved disciple: *the disciple whom Jesus loved is you and me.* The "other disciple" of the Gospel is Everydisciple.

While the beloved disciple is most certainly a historical character from the time of Jesus, it is quite in keeping with the symbolic nature of this Gospel that this disciple should also be an ideal disciple, representing all disciples. The author intended the events in his Gospel to be viewed as symbols with multiple layers of meaning, including both physical and spiritual meanings. The beloved disciple could be both a historical disciple and the ideal disciple—the model for all.

Within the Gospel narrative, the beloved disciple seems to be a model that others would want to imitate. He is often shown to relate to Jesus in an ideal manner, in contrast to the faults of the other disciples. He is the embodiment of discipleship: close to Jesus at the Last Supper, standing beneath his cross, and believing in the risen Christ at the empty tomb. His faith, love, and dedication are presented as attitudes for all of us to imitate. He exemplifies the fact that the most important thing for a disciple is to have a loving relationship with Jesus.

One of the reasons this disciple remains nameless is so that he can take on this universal symbolism. By remaining nameless, he can more easily play the part of representing all of us, who are called to intimacy of life with Christ.

Mary Magdalene: The Witnessing Disciple

Questions to Begin

10 minutes
Use a question or two to get warmed up for the reading.

1 What leader has made you want to follow in his or her footsteps?

2 Recall a time when you have been the bearer of good news to someone. What was that experience like for you?

Father, your Son first entrusted to Mary Magdalene the joyful news of his resurrection. By her prayers and example may we proclaim Christ as our living Lord and one day see him in glory, for he lives and reigns with you and the Holy Spirit, one God, for ever and ever.

Roman Sacramentary, Feast of St. Mary Magdalene

Opening the Bible

10 minutes
*Read the passage aloud. Let individuals take turns reading
paragraphs.*

The Background

There are seven women in the New Testament named Mary.
The word *Magdalene* distinguishes one of them from the others.
Magdalene is most likely an indication that this Mary's hometown
was Magdala, a prosperous town on the Sea of Galilee known for
its fish processing. Mary Magdalene may have been one of Jesus'
earliest followers, since Magdala is located on the western shore
of the Sea of Galilee, between Jesus' hometown of Nazareth and
Capernaum—the fishing village that became the home of Jesus
during his public ministry.

The Reading: Luke 8:1–3; Matthew 27:55–61; 28:1–10; John 20:1–18

The Female Disciples of Jesus

Luke 8:1 Soon afterwards he went on through cities and villages,
proclaiming and bringing the good news of the kingdom of God.
The twelve were with him, 2 as well as some women who had been
cured of evil spirits and infirmities: Mary, called Magdalene, from
whom seven demons had gone out, 3 and Joanna, the wife of Herod's
steward Chuza, and Susanna, and many others, who provided for
them out of their resources.

Mary Magdalene at Jesus' Crucifixion and Burial

Matthew 27:55 Many women were also there, looking on from a
distance; they had followed Jesus from Galilee and had provided for
him. 56 Among them were Mary Magdalene, and Mary the mother
of James and Joseph, and the mother of the sons of Zebedee.

57 When it was evening, there came a rich man from
Arimathea, named Joseph, who was also a disciple of Jesus. 58 He
went to Pilate and asked for the body of Jesus; then Pilate ordered it
to be given to him. 59 So Joseph took the body and wrapped it in a
clean linen cloth 60 and laid it in his own new tomb, which he had
hewn in the rock. He then rolled a great stone to the door of the

tomb and went away. 61 Mary Magdalene and the other Mary were there, sitting opposite the tomb. . . .

Mary Magdalene and the Other Women Meet the Risen Lord

28:1 After the sabbath, as the first day of the week was dawning, Mary Magdalene and the other Mary went to see the tomb. 2 And suddenly there was a great earthquake; for an angel of the Lord, descending from heaven, came and rolled back the stone and sat on it. 3 His appearance was like lightning, and his clothing white as snow. 4 For fear of him the guards shook and became like dead men. 5 But the angel said to the women, "Do not be afraid; I know that you are looking for Jesus who was crucified. 6 He is not here; for he has been raised, as he said. Come, see the place where he lay. 7 Then go quickly and tell his disciples, 'He has been raised from the dead, and indeed he is going ahead of you to Galilee; there you will see him.' This is my message for you." 8 So they left the tomb quickly with fear and great joy, and ran to tell his disciples. 9 Suddenly Jesus met them and said, "Greetings!" And they came to him, took hold of his feet, and worshiped him. 10 Then Jesus said to them, "Do not be afraid; go and tell my brothers to go to Galilee; there they will see me."

Mary Magdalene Becomes the Apostle to the Apostles

John 20:1 Early on the first day of the week, while it was still dark, Mary Magdalene came to the tomb and saw that the stone had been removed from the tomb. 2 So she ran and went to Simon Peter and the other disciple, the one whom Jesus loved, and said to them, "They have taken the Lord out of the tomb, and we do not know where they have laid him." 3 Then Peter and the other disciple set out and went toward the tomb. 4 The two were running together, but the other disciple outran Peter and reached the tomb first. 5 He bent down to look in and saw the linen wrappings lying there, but he did not go in. 6 Then Simon Peter came, following him, and went into the tomb. He saw the linen wrappings lying there, 7 and the cloth that had been on Jesus' head, not lying with the linen wrappings but rolled up in a place by itself. 8 Then the other disciple, who reached the tomb first, also went in, and he saw and believed; 9 for as yet they did not understand the scripture, that he must rise from the dead. 10 Then the disciples returned to their homes.

11 But Mary stood weeping outside the tomb. As she wept, she bent over to look into the tomb; 12 and she saw two angels in white, sitting where the body of Jesus had been lying, one at the head and the other at the feet. 13 They said to her, "Woman, why are you weeping?" She said to them, "They have taken away my Lord, and I do not know where they have laid him." 14 When she had said this, she turned around and saw Jesus standing there, but she did not know that it was Jesus. 15 Jesus said to her, "Woman, why are you weeping? Whom are you looking for?" Supposing him to be the gardener, she said to him, "Sir, if you have carried him away, tell me where you have laid him, and I will take him away." 16 Jesus said to her, "Mary!" She turned and said to him in Hebrew, "Rabbouni!" (which means Teacher). 17 Jesus said to her, "Do not hold on to me, because I have not yet ascended to the Father. But go to my brothers and say to them, 'I am ascending to my Father and your Father, to my God and your God.'" 18 Mary Magdalene went and announced to the disciples, "I have seen the Lord"; and she told them that he had said these things to her.

First Impression

5 minutes
Briefly mention a question you have about the reading or one thing in it that surprised, impressed, delighted, or challenged you. No discussion! Just listen to one another's reactions.

Exploring the Theme

If participants have not read this section already, read it aloud. Otherwise go on to "Questions for Reflection and Discussion."

Luke 8:1–3. One of the surprising features of Jesus' ministry is the presence of female disciples among his followers. This would have been contrary to the Jewish rabbinical customs and considered disgraceful by some. Yet Jesus rarely followed established rules of social correctness in his ministry, and his actions frequently met with disapproval. Luke identifies by name three of the women who traveled with the Twelve and notes that there were "many others" (8:3). These women provided for Jesus and the band of disciples "out of their resources." Some have supposed that these women were primarily concerned with the domestic needs of the men: grinding flour, baking, sewing, and laundering. But "out of their resources" suggests that the women contributed their own property and income so that the disciples could carry on their mission around the countryside. Joanna was the wife of a domestic administrator in Herod's government, and we may also assume that the others were women of means. Yet they were not out of sight, sending money from a distance; they were with Jesus and the Twelve, despite the suspicions they must have raised and the social disapproval of their choice to follow Jesus.

It should be noted that Mary Magdalene is identified solely by her place of origin and not by her relationship to a man, as are other women, like Mary the wife of Clopas (John 19:25) and Mary the mother of Joses (Mark 15:47). This suggests that she was an independent woman, not reliant on a husband, father, or son for her livelihood. This unusual state for a woman of her day was perhaps the result of her severe malady. Luke notes that the women had been cured of evil spirits and infirmities, and Mary Magdalene is further described as one "from whom seven demons had gone out." This suggests that Mary suffered from an extraordinary and chronic emotional or physical disorder. The number seven indicates that her illness was either very severe or recurred frequently. There is absolutely no suggestion in the text that her inner turmoil was the result of, or led to, sexual sin. We might presume that Jesus' healing her from this affliction led her to devote herself to him and his mission.

Matthew 27:55–61. Nowhere in the Gospels is there any suggestion that Jesus regarded the contribution of the female disciples as inferior or subsidiary to that of the men. In fact, in the accounts of his suffering and death, the female disciples seem to show greater courage and determination. Unlike the male disciples, who fear for their lives and flee, the women remain present during Jesus' crucifixion and witness his burial. Matthew notes that there were "many women" who had followed Jesus from Galilee and looked on from a distance at Jesus' crucifixion.

In all four Gospel traditions, the women are witnesses not only of the public ministry of Jesus but also of his death, burial, and resurrection. Though the identification of the women accompanying Jesus varies somewhat from Gospel to Gospel, all four Gospels are unanimous in placing Mary Magdalene at the cross and at the empty tomb. In fact, in all places where the female disciples of Jesus are listed, Mary Magdalene is named first, indicating her position of leadership, at least among the women (Matthew 27:56, 61; 28:1; Mark 15:40, 47; 16:1; Luke 8:2; 24:10). The sole exception is John 19:25, the only passage in which Mary, the mother of Jesus, is listed with the women. Here "his mother" is appropriately named first.

Matthew 28:1–10. In all four Gospels, the female disciples are the first witnesses to Christ's resurrection. Yet each of the Resurrection accounts offers a different list of these women. Matthew's account lists two: "Mary Magdalene and the other Mary." Following the appearance and message of the angel, Jesus himself met and greeted the women as they were running to announce the message of the angel. They approached him in a reverent manner, grasped his feet, and worshiped him. Jesus then commissioned them to go and tell the male disciples to travel to Galilee where they would see him. The authority of these women as bearers of the message of the Resurrection is unchallenged by the men, and so the "eleven disciples" gather in Galilee as they have been instructed.

John 20:1–18. In John's Resurrection account, Mary Magdalene alone is the first recipient of an appearance of the risen Christ, and the first bearer of the good news of his resurrection. As she was weeping at the empty tomb, Jesus revealed himself to her and called her by name. Though she wanted to hold on to him, Jesus told her to go to the apostles with the news. She immediately went to them and announced, "I have seen the Lord" (20:18). She carried out the supreme ministry—that of proclaiming the gospel message of Christ's victory to all the others. She was the first to proclaim that she had seen the risen Lord, that formula of authority by which Paul declared himself to be an apostle (1 Corinthians 9:1). It is this tradition that earned Mary Magdalene the esteemed designation in the early Church, "apostle to the apostles."

Reflections. In his first presentation of Mary Magdalene, Luke notes that seven demons had been cast from her. Yet the Gospel's presentation of Mary Magdalene gives less emphasis to her former state of demon possession and more to her liberated state of discipleship. She is a noteworthy example of the way a healing encounter with Jesus can move people away from being shunned by society and into prominent positions within the community of believers. Mary Magdalene became Jesus' most faithful follower, staying with him as he traveled from Galilee to his crucifixion and burial. At the climax of the Gospel, Mary Magdalene became the first to experience the risen Christ and was commissioned by him to be the premier evangelist. Calling Mary an apostle does not mean that she was one of the Twelve. It means that she was sent out by the risen Lord, like Paul, to proclaim the gospel. Her title, "apostle to the apostles," was given to her by the early patristic writers, repeated by St. Thomas Aquinas in the Middle Ages, and recently revived by contemporary writers, including Pope John Paul II.

Questions for Reflection and Discussion

45 minutes
Choose questions according to your interest and time.

1 Name as many similarities as you can find between the Resurrection account in Matthew's Gospel and that in John's.

2 Compare the response of Mary Magdalene at the tomb of Jesus to that of Peter and the beloved disciple. What is the most significant difference?

3 Why do you think Mary did not recognize the risen Jesus at first? Why did his calling her name have such an effect on her?

4 After Mary Magdalene was healed by Jesus of her seven demons, her whole life changed. What do you suppose might have been the most dramatic aspect of that change?

5 How have the readings and commentary changed or enhanced your understanding of Mary Magdalene? Does the change make her more significant for you?

6 After Mary Magdalene recognized the risen Christ, he told her not to "hold on" to him (John 20:17). Compare Mary's desire to hold on to Jesus to your own desire to hold on to those you love.

7 **Focus question.** How could Mary Magdalene be a model of discipleship for you? What aspects of her discipleship would you like to imitate?

Prayer to Close

*10 minutes
Use this approach—or create your own!*

♦ Lead the group in the following prayer.

Leader: As our savior, Jesus heals our infirmities, releases us from bondage, and restores us to new life. Let us call upon his saving power.

Leader: For all those in need of Christ's healing . . .
All: Unbind them, Lord, and let them go free.

Leader: For all those in need of Christ's release from bondage or oppression . . .
All: Unbind them, Lord, and let them go free.

Leader: For all those who have died, that they may experience new life in Christ forever . . .
All: Unbind them, Lord, and let them go free.

Leader: Lord Jesus, you are our healer, redeemer, and savior. Help your people in their needs, and come to our aid with your liberating grace. Amen.

Between Discussions

Who Is Mary Magdalene, Really?

Mary Magdalene has been an intriguing character throughout Christian history. Her prominence among the women of the Gospels has led many to speculate about her identity and to expand her persona beyond what the Gospels tell us. Often in Christian art and films, she has been confused with unnamed women in the Gospels, usually either with the sinful woman who anointed the feet of Jesus (Luke 7:37) or with the adulterous woman forgiven by Jesus (John 8:3). More recent speculation has made the incredible claim that she was Jesus' wife. None of these purported roles of Mary Magdalene—as adulterer, prostitute, or spouse of Jesus—has any support from historical evidence or indications in the New Testament.

Was Mary Magdalene a prostitute? In Western Christianity, the predominant image we have of Mary Magdalene is of a scarlet-cloaked, beautiful woman with long, loose hair. She is depicted at the feet of Jesus, either anointing his feet and drying them with her hair or kneeling at the cross of Jesus, weeping for her sins. As expressed in Western Christian art and literature, she is the embodiment of feminine sensuality, sexuality, and sin. She is the prostitute who, upon meeting Jesus Christ, repented of her sinful past and devoted herself solely to love and devotion to him.

We look in vain for this conception of Mary Magdalene in the four Gospels. Nowhere in the New Testament do we find Mary the prostitute, adulterer, or sinner. Yet, after the first few centuries of the Church, Mary Magdalene—the chief female disciple, beloved friend of Jesus, and first to announce the gospel to the apostles—was transformed into a prostitute.

Mary Magdalene's harlotization probably resulted from confusion of Mary Magdalene with other women in the Gospels. Mary Magdalene is one of seven women in the New Testament named Mary. The Church in the earliest centuries did a good job of keeping the Marys separate, and the Orthodox Church and Byzantine Catholics have always maintained separate feasts for Mary of Magdala and Mary of Bethany. It was only in the sixth-century West that the figure of Mary Magdalene was fused with other Marys and with unnamed sinners in the Gospels. Pope Gregory the Great, in a homily given in AD 591, collapsed three distinct Gospel figures—Mary Magdalene, Mary of Bethany, and the unnamed sinful woman who anointed the feet of Jesus—into one individual. He declared, "She whom Luke calls the sinful woman, whom John calls Mary, we believe to be the Mary from whom seven devils were ejected." The identification seemed to answer questions posed at the time about the relationship of these women in the Gospels and may have reflected a common misunderstanding that resulted from confusing the accounts in the Gospels of Luke and John.

In the seventh chapter of his Gospel, Luke describes the encounter of Jesus with "a woman in the city, who was a sinner" (Luke 7:37). Jesus had been invited to dine at the home of a religious leader. During the meal, a woman entered the dining room, bathed Jesus' feet with her tears, dried his feet with her hair, kissed his feet, and anointed them with ointment from her alabaster jar (Luke 7:38). Despite the host's disapproval, Jesus admired the woman's great love and forgave her many sins (Luke 7:47). Immediately after this account, Luke introduces Mary Magdalene as a woman from whom seven demons had gone out (Luke 8:2). The sequence of the two accounts led to confusion and misidentification of these two individuals. At a time when women's sins were often labeled as sexual sins, Mary Magdalene was branded a prostitute.

In the twelfth chapter of John's Gospel, another Mary, the sister of Martha and Lazarus, is shown at the feet of Jesus when Jesus goes to their home in Bethany. This Mary "anointed Jesus' feet, and wiped them with her hair" (John 12:3). Through the centuries, this Mary of Bethany was often mistaken for Mary Magdalene, who was associated with the sinful woman of Luke's account. It was thought that the Mary who anointed the feet of Jesus and wiped them with her hair was called Mary Magdalene in Luke's Gospel and Mary of Bethany in John's Gospel. Pope Gregory identified these three figures—the sinful woman, Mary Magdalene, and Mary of Bethany—as the same person because it seemed to make sense of the confusion caused by the similarities of these three in the various Gospels.

To view the homily of Pope Gregory as an act of malice would be a gross misrepresentation. But regrettably, the misidentification stuck, and Mary Magdalene was thereafter viewed as a great sinner and penitent. Her image as the sinner-saint grew, which is one of the reasons why so many people through the ages have been attracted to her. She provided hope that even great sinners can be forgiven and their lives renewed by the merciful Christ.

Was Mary Magdalene the wife of Jesus? In recent years, the pendulum of popular opinion has begun to swing in a different direction in regard to Mary Magdalene. Rather than branding her as a prostitute, recent theorists have proposed that she was Jesus' wife.

Speculative writers have noted that Mary Magdalene is not associated with any man besides Jesus in the Gospels and that she is always the first listed among his female disciples. John's text, depicting her as the first witness to the Resurrection and reporting on Jesus' insistence that she not hold on to him (John 20:17), suggests to many that there was a uniquely loving relationship between Jesus and Mary Magdalene. When this Gospel data is added to the fact that it was unusual at the time for a Jewish teacher to remain unmarried, it is a short leap for some to suggest that the two were joined in matrimony.

The theory also relies heavily on two texts from the second- and third-century heretical movement called Gnosticism. These texts are called "gospels" because they contain narratives about Jesus, although the Church never recognized them as authentic expressions of the gospel, or "Good News," about Jesus Christ. *The Gospel of Philip* describes Mary as a "companion" of Jesus and states that the disciples complained that Jesus kissed her. But neither reference establishes a sexual, romantic, or marital relationship. *The Gospel of Mary* claims that Mary Magdalene was the recipient of a special revelation from Jesus not given to the other apostles and that Jesus loved her more than them.

These gnostic texts are highly mystical and symbolic and are filled with spiritual imagery. Yet they include nothing of historical value about Jesus. They also contain countless misrepresentations of the true nature of Christ, which is why they were never considered part of the inspired canon of Scripture. And, in any case, the esoteric references in these gnostic writings refer to a spiritual relationship between Jesus and Mary—not matrimony.

Not in any of the volumes of Christian writings from the Church's early centuries, including the Bible, is there any text that indicates that Jesus was married or that Mary Magdalene was his wife. Though nowhere in the Gospels is it stated that Jesus remained single, there are plenty of places where the evangelists could have made reference to his marital state if indeed he had been married. His itinerant lifestyle and the urgency of his mission were not conducive to marriage and family life.

Recent speculation that Jesus and Mary Magdalene were husband and wife is just that—speculation. The theories are fascinating to many, but the evidence proposed does not stand up to scrutiny, and the canonical Gospels suggest no such thing. It is better to honor Mary Magdalene for who she truly was, rather than try to sensationalize her status with bogus theorizing.

So, who is Mary Magdalene, really? Mary Magdalene is a great saint and worthy model for all of us. She was a woman bound by the forces of evil whom Jesus healed. Jesus gave her a new life, and she followed him with profound gratitude and love, so much so that she was the first witness to his resurrection and the one who proclaimed the good news to all the others. Though recent conspiracy theorists charge that Church leaders maligned her for their own purposes, the tribute shown to Mary Magdalene through the ages demonstrates the opposite. She has been honored by the Church through the ages as a noble saint, and her feast is celebrated by the universal church on July 22. There are churches named after her all over the world.

Mary Magdalene serves as an inspiration for us far more in these ways than by suggestions and flimsy arguments that she was the wife of Jesus or a repentant prostitute. Hopefully, current biblical scholarship can reverse centuries of misrepresentation of Mary Magdalene in the West. Perhaps Mary Magdalene, properly identified and honored, can become again a great saint for the church of the twenty-first century.

MARY OF NAZARETH: THE MODEL DISCIPLE

Questions to Begin

10 minutes
Use a question or two to get warmed up for the reading.

1 When has your life taken a different direction than you had planned?

2 What is one thing your mother or father taught you about life that you will always remember?

In the faith of his humble handmaid, the Gift of God found the acceptance he had awaited from the beginning of time. She whom the Almighty made "full of grace" responds by offering her whole being: "Behold I am the handmaid of the Lord; let it be [done] to me according to your word."

Catechism of the Catholic Church, section 2617

Opening the Bible

10 minutes
Read the passage aloud. Let individuals take turns reading paragraphs.

The Background

Mary of Nazareth, the mother of Jesus, is portrayed in the Gospels of Luke and John as the model disciple. Throughout her life she exemplifies the teachings of Jesus about what it is to be a true disciple. The first readings from Luke describe Mary's call to be the mother of Christ and her response to God's word throughout her life. The Annunciation to Mary could be described as a call story, with similarities to the call of the disciples in the early stages of Jesus' adult ministry. Mary responds generously to God's word and then dedicates her life to listening to it and doing it. The selection from John's Gospel shows Mary present at Cana as she prepares the way for Jesus' first public miracle. The Scriptures demonstrate that Mary was with Jesus from the beginning of his life to the very end. The final selection shows Mary with the apostles in the upper room in Jerusalem, awaiting the coming of the Holy Spirit. Among the many believers gathered in Jerusalem at Pentecost, Mary was an essential member of the infant Church. She remains at the heart of the community of Jesus' disciples, following in the way of Jesus.

The Reading: Luke 1:26–45; 8:11–15, 19–21; John 2:1–11; Acts 1:12–14

Responding Wholeheartedly to God's Word

Luke 1:26 In the sixth month the angel Gabriel was sent by God to a town in Galilee called Nazareth, 27 to a virgin engaged to a man whose name was Joseph, of the house of David. The virgin's name was Mary. 28 And he came to her and said, "Greetings, favored one! The Lord is with you." 29 But she was much perplexed by his words and pondered what sort of greeting this might be. 30 The angel said to her, "Do not be afraid, Mary, for you have found favor with God. 31 And now, you will conceive in your womb and bear a son, and you will name him Jesus. 32 He will be great, and will be called the Son of the Most High, and the Lord God will give to him the throne of his ancestor David. 33 He will reign over the house of Jacob forever, and of his kingdom there will be no end."

34 Mary said to the angel, "How can this be, since I am a virgin?" 35 The angel said to her, "The Holy Spirit will come upon you, and the power of the Most High will overshadow you; therefore the child to be born will be holy; he will be called Son of God. 36 And now, your relative Elizabeth in her old age has also conceived a son; and this is the sixth month for her who was said to be barren. 37 For nothing will be impossible with God." 38 Then Mary said, "Here am I, the servant of the Lord; let it be with me according to your word." Then the angel departed from her.

39 In those days Mary set out and went with haste to a Judean town in the hill country, 40 where she entered the house of Zechariah and greeted Elizabeth. 41 When Elizabeth heard Mary's greeting, the child leaped in her womb. And Elizabeth was filled with the Holy Spirit 42 and exclaimed with a loud cry, "Blessed are you among women, and blessed is the fruit of your womb. 43 And why has this happened to me, that the mother of my Lord comes to me? 44 For as soon as I heard the sound of your greeting, the child in my womb leaped for joy. 45 And blessed is she who believed that there would be a fulfillment of what was spoken to her by the Lord."

Hearing and Doing the Word of God

8:11 "Now the parable is this: The seed is the word of God. 12 The ones on the path are those who have heard; then the devil comes and takes away the word from their hearts, so that they may not believe and be saved. 13 The ones on the rock are those who, when they hear the word, receive it with joy. But these have no root; they believe only for a while and in a time of testing fall away. 14 As for what fell among the thorns, these are the ones who hear; but as they go on their way, they are choked by the cares and riches and pleasures of life, and their fruit does not mature. 15 But as for that in the good soil, these are the ones who, when they hear the word, hold it fast in an honest and good heart, and bear fruit with patient endurance." . . .

19 Then his mother and his brothers came to him, but they could not reach him because of the crowd. 20 And he was told, "Your mother and your brothers are standing outside, wanting to see you." 21 But he said to them, "My mother and my brothers are those who hear the word of God and do it."

Mary and the Disciples at a Wedding Feast

John 2:1 On the third day there was a wedding in Cana of Galilee, and the mother of Jesus was there. 2 Jesus and his disciples had also been invited to the wedding. 3 When the wine gave out, the mother of Jesus said to him, "They have no wine." 4 And Jesus said to her, "Woman, what concern is that to you and to me? My hour has not yet come." 5 His mother said to the servants, "Do whatever he tells you."

6 Now standing there were six stone water jars for the Jewish rites of purification, each holding twenty or thirty gallons. 7 Jesus said to them, "Fill the jars with water." And they filled them up to the brim. 8 He said to them, "Now draw some out, and take it to the chief steward." So they took it. 9 When the steward tasted the water that had become wine, and did not know where it came from (though the servants who had drawn the water knew), the steward called the bridegroom 10 and said to him, "Everyone serves the good wine first, and then the inferior wine after the guests have become drunk. But you have kept the good wine until now." 11 Jesus did this, the first of his signs, in Cana of Galilee, and revealed his glory; and his disciples believed in him.

Mary and the Apostles Await the Holy Spirit

Acts 1:12 Then they returned to Jerusalem from the mount called Olivet, which is near Jerusalem, a sabbath day's journey away. 13 When they had entered the city, they went to the room upstairs where they were staying, Peter, and John, and James, and Andrew, Philip and Thomas, Bartholomew and Matthew, James son of Alphaeus, and Simon the Zealot, and Judas son of James. 14 All these were constantly devoting themselves to prayer, together with certain women, including Mary the mother of Jesus, as well as his brothers.

First Impression

5 minutes
Briefly mention a question you have about the reading or one thing in it that surprised, impressed, delighted, or challenged you. No discussion! Just listen to one another's reactions.

Exploring the Theme

If participants have not read this section already, read it aloud.
Otherwise go on to "Questions for Reflection and Discussion."

Luke 1:26–45. When God called Mary through the angel to be the mother of his Son, her reply was that of a disciple who lives by faith. Though what God was asking of her would bring turbulence and upheaval into her life, Mary accepted her calling with confidence in the God she had come to know as trustworthy. Though we may imagine the scene to be peaceful and serene, the call to Mary was truly unnerving. The words of the angel, "Do not be afraid"—the same words that God spoke to Mary's ancestors in Israel through the ages—were offered to reassure her and offer her hope.

Mary passed from fear, through puzzlement, to wholehearted acceptance: "Here am I, the servant of the Lord; let it be with me according to your word" (1:38). This complete giving of herself to God, to whatever God asked of her, was the self-abandonment of discipleship. It is the calling of every Christian disciple. This self-denial, as consent to God's will for one's life, is also a discovery of one's truest self. When we recognize that the direction of our lives is planned by the One who knows us best, we realize that his plan always corresponds to our heart's deepest and most noble desires. Responding to God's call, like Mary, always means opening our lives more widely to admit the God of all possibility.

Mary's consent to God's plan for her also set in motion God's plan for the world. As St. Augustine said: "Mary did not have intercourse and conceive; instead she *believed* and conceived." Through her one act of faith and total self-gift to God, Mary conceived and became the birth giver of God. Through hearing the word of God in faith and giving herself wholly to God, Mary became the first and most perfect disciple.

The words of Elizabeth express the twofold tribute that we give to Mary, as both mother of Christ and model of discipleship. First, she honors Mary as the bearer of Christ: "Blessed are you among women, and blessed is the fruit of your womb" (1:42). Second, she honors Mary as the ideal disciple: "Blessed is she who believed that there would be a fulfillment of what was spoken to her by the Lord" (1:45). Mary listens to God's word and trusts that God will bring about what he has promised.

Luke 8:11–15, 19–21. After presenting the parable of the sower and the seed, Jesus explains that the seed is the word of God. The good soil is the true disciples: "These are the ones who, when they hear the word, hold it fast in an honest and good heart, and bear fruit with patient endurance" (8:15). The exemplary disciples are those who listen to God's word, cherish it, and bring forth results.

A few verses later, Jesus talks of his mother and praises her for being one of those who will "hear the word of God and do it" (8:21). Mary allowed God's word to bear fruit in her life because she nurtured the word in her heart. As the Gospel writer says of her in the infancy accounts: "Mary treasured all these words and pondered them in her heart" (2:19, 51). Mary is family to Jesus not just because she bore him in her womb but because she listened and responded to God's word. It is this kind of disciple who is included in the family of Jesus. When a woman in the crowd shouted out to Jesus, "Blessed is the womb that bore you and the breasts that nursed you!" Jesus replied, "Blessed rather are those who hear the word of God and obey it" (11:27–28). Mary did exactly this, which makes her the model for us all—the ideal Christian disciple.

But Mary is not only the model disciple; she is still mother—not only of Jesus but of all disciples. Since she is part of Jesus' new family of faith by her response of discipleship, she is mother to all those who enter into this family through discipleship. As mother of Jesus by blood and mother of disciples by faith, she not only gives us the best example but cares for us with motherly concern.

John 2:1–11. In John's Gospel, Mary's final words are these: "Do whatever he tells you" (2:5). Doing what Jesus asks, obeying God's word through him—this is true discipleship. Genuine obedience, however, has nothing to do with unthinking compliance or forced submission; obedience means truly listening. Mary demonstrates that obedience means listening to God's word, savoring that word, and then responding wholeheartedly. Through her example of listening and keeping God's word, she taught all the disciples of Jesus to do the same. Thanks to the example and intervention of Mary, "his disciples believed in him" (2:11).

Acts 1:12–14. When Mary is mentioned for the last time in the New Testament narratives, she is with the apostles, praying and waiting for the coming of the Holy Spirit at Pentecost (1:14). By depicting her after the earthly life of Jesus had ended—here on the first page of Church history—Luke shows that Mary is at the heart of the emerging Church.

The early Church in Acts is characterized in several ways. The members were devoted to the apostles' teachings; they were joined together in one fellowship; they were bound in Christ through celebrating the Eucharist; and they were united in prayer (2:42). This is the community of disciples for which Mary is both model and mother.

Reflections. Being a disciple of Jesus involves both a vertical and a horizontal dimension. It entails a personal relationship with him as well as a bond of unity with other disciples. Discipleship means being united in heart and mind with both Jesus and fellow disciples, being part of a universal family. Mary, mother and disciple, is at the heart of that new family of God. With Mary, the Church will always listen to God's word, ponder it with holy hearts, and, empowered by the Holy Spirit, act on that word to bear fruit in the world.

45 minutes
Choose questions according to your interest and time.

---

1 In what way does Mary's life exemplify the good soil of the true disciple (Luke 8:15)?

---

2 Why is discipleship more important to Jesus than blood ties (Luke 8:20–21)?

---

3 In what way does this study of Mary as the first and most perfect disciple change or expand your understanding of the role she might play in your life?

---

4 In what way have you discovered that self-denial leads to discovery of your truest self?

---

5 In what way have you become family to Jesus (Luke 8:21)? What does it mean for you to live as a member of his family?

6 What is the real meaning of obedience to God? Where in your life could you make a better response to the counsel of Mary: "Do whatever he tells you" (John 2:5)?

7 Why has Mary been given the title "Mother of the Church"? What does it mean for Mary to be the mother of Christians? In what way do you experience her as your mother?

8 How is discipleship to Jesus both a personal relationship to him and a communal relationship with his other followers? Which of these dimensions of your discipleship needs the most work?

9 **Focus question.** How could Mary be a model of discipleship for you? Which of her qualities would you most want to apply to your own life?

Prayer to Close

10 minutes
Use this approach—or create your own!

♦ **Leader:** Lord God, you called Mary of Nazareth to carry your incarnate Word in her womb and to bring him forth into our world. May she be our model as we receive your word in our hearts and become bearers of your word to those around us.

Let us respond to each invocation of the litany "Pray for us."

Mary, beloved daughter of God our Father . . .
Mary, tender mother of Jesus Christ, the Son . . .
Mary, sacred temple of the Holy Spirit . . .
Mary, ark of the covenant . . .
Mary, tabernacle of God's presence . . .
Mary, bearer of the Word of God . . .
Mary, model of Christian discipleship . . .
Mary, queen of apostles . . .
Mary, mother of the Church . . .

Hail Mary, full of grace . . .

Suggestions for Bible Discussion Groups

Like a camping trip, a Bible discussion group works best if you agree on where you're going and how you intend to get there. Many groups use their first meeting to talk over such questions. Here is a checklist of issues, with bits of advice from people who have experience in Bible discussions. (A planning discussion will go more smoothly if the leaders have thought through the following issues beforehand.)

Agree on your purpose. Are you getting together to gain wisdom and direction for your lives? to finally get acquainted with the Bible? to support one another in following Christ? to encourage those who are exploring—or reexploring—the Church? for other reasons?

Agree on attitudes. For example: "We're all beginners here." "We're here to help one another understand and respond to God's word." "We're not here to offer counseling or direction to one another." "We want to read Scripture prayerfully." What do *you* wish to emphasize? Make it explicit!

Agree on ground rules. Barbara J. Fleischer, in her useful book *Facilitating for Growth,* recommends that a group clearly state its approach to the following:

- *Preparation.* Do we agree to read the material and prepare answers to the questions before each meeting?
- *Attendance.* What kind of priority will we give to our meetings?
- *Self-revelation.* Are we willing to help the others in the group gradually get to know us—our weaknesses as well as our strengths, our needs as well as our gifts?
- *Listening.* Will we commit ourselves to listen to one another?
- *Confidentiality.* Will we keep everything that is shared *with* the group *in* the group?
- *Discretion.* Will we refrain from sharing about the faults and sins of people who are not in the group?
- *Encouragement and support.* Will we give as well as receive?
- *Participation.* Will we give each person the time and opportunity to make a contribution?

You could probably take a pen and draw a circle around *listening* and *confidentiality.* Those two points are especially important.

The following items could be added to Fleischer's list:

♦ *Relationship with parish.* Is our group part of the adult faith-formation program? independent but operating with the express approval of the pastor? not a parish-based group?

♦ *New members.* Will we let new members join us once we have begun the six weeks of discussions?

Agree on housekeeping.

♦ *When will we meet?*

♦ *How often will we meet?* Meeting weekly or every other week is best if you can manage it. William Riley remarks, "Meetings once a month are too distant from each other for the threads of the last session not to be lost" (*The Bible Study Group: An Owner's Manual*).

♦ *How long will each meeting run?*

♦ *Where will we meet?*

♦ *Is any setup needed?* Christine Dodd writes that "the problem with meeting in a place like a church hall is that it can be very soul-destroying," given the cold, impersonal feel of many church facilities. If you have to meet in a church facility, Dodd recommends doing something to make the area homey (*Making Scripture Work*).

♦ *Who will host the meetings?* Leaders and hosts are not necessarily the same people.

♦ *Will we have refreshments?* Who will provide them? Don Cousins and Judson Poling make this recommendation: "Serve refreshments if you like, but save snacks and other foods for the end of the meeting to minimize distractions" (*Leader's Guide 1*).

♦ *What about child care?* Most experienced leaders of Bible discussion groups discourage bringing infants or other children to adult Bible discussions.

Agree on leadership. You need someone to facilitate— to keep the discussion on track, to see that everyone has a chance to speak, to help the group stay on schedule. Rena Duff, editor of the newsletter *Sharing God's Word Today,* recommends having two or three people take turns leading the discussions.

It's okay if the leader is not an expert on the Bible. You have this Six Weeks book as a guide, and if questions come up that no one can answer, you can delegate a participant to do a little research between meetings. Perhaps your parish priest or someone on the pastoral staff of your parish could offer advice. Or help may be available from your diocesan catechetical office or a local Catholic college or seminary.

It's important for the leader to set an example of listening, to draw out the quieter members (and occasionally restrain the more vocal ones), to move the group on when it gets stuck, to get the group back on track when the discussion moves away from the topic, and to restate and summarize what the group is learning. Sometimes the leader needs to remind the members of their agreements. An effective group leader is enthusiastic about the topic and the discussions and sets an example of learning from others and of using resources for growing in understanding.

As a discussion group matures, other members of the group will increasingly share in doing all these things on their own initiative.

Bible discussion is an opportunity to experience the fulfillment of Jesus' promise "Where two or three are gathered in my name, I am there among them" (Matthew 18:20). Put your discussion group in Jesus' hands. Pray for the guidance of the Spirit. And have a great time exploring God's word together!

Suggestions for Individuals

Y ou can use this book just as well for individual study as for group discussion. While discussing the Bible with other people can be a rich experience, there are advantages to reading on your own. For example:

♦ You can focus on the points that interest you most.

♦ You can go at your own pace.

♦ You can be completely relaxed and unashamedly honest in your answers to all the questions, since you don't have to share them with anyone!

My suggestions for using this book on your own are these:

♦ Don't skip "Questions to Begin" or "First Impression."

♦ Take your time on "Questions for Reflection and Discussion." While a group will probably not have enough time to work on all the questions, you can allow yourself the time to consider all of them if you are using the book by yourself.

♦ After reading "Exploring the Theme," go back and reread the Scripture text before answering the Questions for Reflection and Discussion.

♦ Take the time to look up all the parenthetical Scripture references.

♦ Read additional sections of Scripture related to the excerpts in this book. For example, read the portions of Scripture that come before and after the sections that form the readings in this Six Weeks book. You will understand the readings better by viewing them in context in the Bible.

♦ Since you control the pace, give yourself plenty of opportunities to reflect on the meaning of the Scripture passages for you. Let your reading be an opportunity for these words to become God's words to you.

Resources

Bibles

The following editions of the Bible contain the full set of biblical books recognized by the Catholic Church, along with a great deal of useful explanatory material:

- ◆ The Catholic Study Bible (Oxford University Press), which uses the text of the New American Bible
- ◆ The Catholic Bible: Personal Study Edition (Oxford University Press), which also uses the text of the New American Bible
- ◆ The New Jerusalem Bible, the regular (not the reader's) edition (Doubleday)

Books, Web Sites, and Other Resources

- ◆ Dietrich Bonhoeffer, *The Cost of Discipleship* (New York: Touchstone, 1995).
- ◆ Georg Fischer, SJ, and Martin Hasitschka, SJ, *The Call of the Disciple: The Bible on Following Christ* (New York: Paulist Press, 1999).
- ◆ Dennis Sweetland, *Our Journey with Jesus: Discipleship According to Luke–Acts* (Wilmington, DE: Michael Glazier, 1990).
- ◆ Dennis Sweetland, *Our Journey with Jesus: Discipleship According to Mark* (Wilmington, DE: Michael Glazier, 1987).

How has Scripture had an impact on your life? Was this book helpful to you in your study of the Bible? Please send comments, suggestions, and personal experiences to Kevin Perrotta, General Editor, Editorial Department, Loyola Press, 3441 N. Ashland Ave., Chicago, IL 60657.